GLAMORGAN

SHERIFFS

GLAMORGAN SHERIFFS

Biographical Notes
on Sheriffs 1966–1993
and
Lists of Sheriffs
from the Twelfth Century
to the Present Day

Edited by

PATRICIA MOORE

Published on behalf of the
Glamorgan County History Trust
by
University of Wales Press
Cardiff
1995

British Library Cataloguing-in-Publication Data.
A catalogue record for this book is available from the British Library.

ISBN 0-7083-1264-0

Typeset in 11/12pt Sabon at the University of Wales Press
Jacket design by Design Principle, Cardiff
Printed in Great Britain by the Alden Press, Oxford

Contents

Foreword

by Sir Michael Llewellyn

As Chairman of the Glamorgan County History Trust, it gives me great pleasure to write a foreword to *Glamorgan Sheriffs*, a distinguished companion to the *High Sheriffs of the County of Glamorgan from 1541 to 1966* published in 1966 by my good friend George Williams, then High Sheriff of Glamorgan. I am delighted to recognize the fact that his son Owain maintained a fine family tradition by serving as High Sheriff of Mid Glamorgan in 1985.

George Williams, Dr Richard John and Patricia Moore were the driving forces behind the earlier volume, and I am delighted to record their continued presence among us. Dr John, now 90, but then the penultimate holder of the distinguished office of Clerk of the Peace of Glamorgan, has always been a devoted supporter of the History Trust and, indeed, it was thanks to Sir Cennydd Traherne and to him that the Trust was revived in 1953. Thus ensued the completion of the six volumes of the *Glamorgan County History*. Mrs Moore, after twenty years as County Archivist, continues to add to our wealth of knowledge of the county's history, and I pay a warm tribute to her persistence in compiling the records of some sixty-eight High Sheriffs.

The earlier volume records the changes then developing in the industrial and social structure of Glamorgan, the pace of which has accelerated in the past thirty years. We take for granted the undoubted burden that falls on the shoulders of High Sheriffs in the ever challenging and changing times of county and shire administration. Nevertheless, this ancient office, which proudly proclaims its antiquity, can contribute enormously in establishing continuity in the civic changes around us as we inexorably approach the millennium. Whilst it is good to see shire designations and traditions reappearing elsewhere in Wales, the titular loss of the ancient shire of Glamorgan is to be regretted and I warmly acknowledge the financial sponsorship we have so readily received from the county councils of the old Glamorgan, Mid, South and West Glamorgan.

Foreword

I hope this volume will be as well received as its precursor and will give pride to the holders of the ancient office and, equally importantly, will be a vital source of information for the social historians of the twenty-first century.

No publication of the Trust can pass without a warm word of thanks for the assistance and help I so readily receive from Emeritus Professor Glanmor Williams and Professor Ralph Griffiths, and it is in no formal sense that I record my appreciation to them.

1 August 1994

Michael Llewellyn,
Glebe House.
Penmaen,
West Glamorgan.

The Trustees of the History Trust wish to take this opportunity to express their appreciation for the work of their late Chairman, Sir Michael Llewellyn, Bart., himself a former High Sheriff of West Glamorgan, who passed away on 8 September 1994. His wise and genial guidance as Chairman since 1989 will be sorely missed.

Preface

This book is about the office of Sheriff, or High Sheriff, as it is also termed, in the historic county of Glamorgan and in its three successor counties created in 1974. It records the individuals who have held that office. Early sheriffs are listed by name, date and place of origin only, but from 1966 onwards the sixty-eight sheriffs of the area are described in short biographical notes, with accompanying photographs. Other illustrations help to show the present functions of the sheriff.

The present compilation owes much to a similar volume, *High Sheriffs of the County of Glamorgan from 1541 to 1966*, which I was asked to prepare for publication in 1966 for Mr George Williams of Llanharan House to mark his shrieval year. That work contained notes and pedigrees of the landowning families which had provided sheriffs through the centuries, generation after generation. It also alluded to the very few industrial dynasties which had provided sheriffs by reason of their wealth and subsequent purchase of land.

When I started to prepare the present volume at the invitation of the Chairman and Committee of the Glamorgan County History Trust, the appropriate format which suggested itself was very different from that of the 1966 volume. The background to today's shrievalty is no longer the same. There has been considerable economic and social change, and the historic Glamorgan was, in 1974, divided into three new counties: Mid Glamorgan, South Glamorgan and West Glamorgan. This book looks at each sheriff individually, and so takes the form of short biographical notes; these aim to reveal the diversity, and yet the similarities, which mark the background of the men and women who have served the office in recent years.

My thanks are due to the sixty-eight former sheriffs featured in this book, who have provided the biographical information and have answered further questions with great patience and forbearance. Likewise I am grateful to their wives, or in some cases, their widows, as well as family members and secretaries who have taken telephone messages, confirmed details or looked for relevant photographs. The material thus supplied has gone to form the main text of the book.

Preface

The Under Sheriff of the Bailiwick of Glamorgan, Mr John Otto-Jones, kindly agreed to write a short note on the duties of his office. He has also given me invaluable assistance and guidance generally. I am grateful to him, and to the Under Sheriff of the Bailiwick of Swansea, Mr John Edmund.

Work on this book started before my retirement from the post of Glamorgan Archivist. I am glad of this opportunity to express my gratitude to those members of the staff of the Glamorgan Record Office who have assisted in various ways, in particular Michael Wilcox, an archivist whose painstaking research has been most helpful, not to mention his care of the photographs assembled for publication. Mrs Ann Sefton carried out the photocopying and Mrs Colleen Abson undertook the initial typing, assisted by Mrs Karen Jones.

I am grateful to Miss Susan Beckley for her assistance, both when she was on my staff within the Glamorgan Archive Service, and latterly as County Archivist of the now independent West Glamorgan County Record Office. The staff of that office, too, have been very helpful.

A work of this kind depends on a host of people who have checked or supplied details: the Clerks to the Lieutenancy through Barbara Edwards, Pat Davies and Nora Davies; Julia Davenport of the Priory for Wales of the Most Venerable Order of the Hospital of St John of Jerusalem; Bryn Owen of The Welch Regiment Museum, Cardiff Castle; David Williamson of Debrett; S. J. Holt, Clerk to a number of London Livery Companies; the South Wales Police Authority for information regarding the award of the Shrieval Cup; the Registrars' Departments of the University of Wales; Colin Linnard, former Secretary to the Chairman of Glamorgan, later Mid Glamorgan, County Council, and his successor, John Asquith, assisted by Margaret Ellmes. To all these I offer my thanks.

It was Mr George Williams who first kindled my interest in the shrievalty, and I am grateful to him for a happy association in the production of the 1966 book and for allowing the list which appeared in that publication to be used again in this volume. The Glamorgan History Trust has also given permission for the list of the sheriffs of the medieval Lordship of Glamorgan which appeared in volume III of the *Glamorgan County History* series to be included in this work, thus taking the coverage back to the beginning of the twelfth century.

The work could not have proceeded without the helpful support of Emeritus Professor Glanmor Williams, General Editor of the *Glamorgan County History*, of Professor Ralph Griffiths, Secretary to the Trust, and of Mr Michael Rush, its Treasurer. My particular thanks are due to Sir Michael Llewellyn, Chairman of the Trust, for his interest and support throughout the project; he was the initiator of the proposal for the present publication.

From the University of Wales Press, in the persons of Susan Jenkins and Ceinwen Jones, I have received every possible assistance. I am grateful to them for guiding the publication through the press in all its aspects.

Finally, my thanks are due to my husband for much practical assistance, especially in proof-reading, and for his ever ready encouragement and support.

2 August 1994   PATRICIA MOORE

Acknowledgements

The author wishes to thank the photographers listed below for their permission, in all cases readily given, to reproduce the photographs on the pages indicated.

Richard Bosworth, 40; British Steel, 10; Ellis Photography, Newport, 54; Glamorgan County Council, 2; *Glamorgan Gazette*, 59; Hills Welsh Press Ltd, Cardiff, 29; Justin B. Ingram, Bridgend, 16; Peter S. Jones, Gowerton, 74; Malcolm Lewis, Abergavenny, 14; David Mathias, Cardiff, 42; Mid Glamorgan County Council, 25; David Morgan, Kenfig Hill, 26; PRT Photography, Swansea, 77; M. D. Smith, Ynystawe, 72; South Glamorgan County Council, 56; South Wales Police Authority, 11b; STP Photography, Cardiff, 32, 52, 53, 61, 71; Ronald Turner, Cardiff, 47; VIP Photography, Cardiff, 33; West Glamorgan County Council, 3, 6, 7; *Western Mail & Echo*, 58; Peter Wilson, Barry, 57.

Every effort has been made to trace the copyright holders of photographs in this volume. In case of any query, please contact the publishers.

The Shrievalty in Glamorgan

The Shrievalty Association of Great Britain chose the year 1992 to mark the millennium of the shrievalty in England and to celebrate the continuity of an office which was already well established in the Anglo-Saxon shires by the end of the tenth century. The office of sheriff is the oldest surviving secular office in the land.

In the eleventh century the shrievalty was taken over by the Normans after their conquest of England, and it was the Normans who introduced it into Wales. They penetrated into the country along the coastal lowlands and river valleys of south and mid Wales. Dispossessing the native Welsh rulers, they established their dominium, creating Marcher lordships, which were frontier zones where the Marcher lord exercised considerable independence from the Crown.

The sheriffs of English shires, who were principal officials bearing responsibility to the Crown, are more fully documented than the sheriffs of the medieval lordship of Glamorgan. In Wales fewer records have survived, but sheriffs appear as powerful officials of the Marcher lord. They held his courts, enforced law and order, ensured the collection of his dues and are formally recorded as witnesses to important events and transactions within the lordship. They could, and did, use force when violent situations demanded it. The names of those who held the office of sheriff during the Middle Ages are, almost without exception, of Norman or, later, English origin, indicative of the background of the ruling class. A few were already significant landholders within the lordship, and names such as Turbervill reappear in the shrieval list in later centuries.

By the early sixteenth century the lordship of Glamorgan had come into the possession of the Crown. The last two sheriffs to hold office in the lordship before the Acts of Union, each in turn appointed for life, were Charles and Henry Somerset, father and son, Earls of Worcester, forebears of the later Dukes of Beaufort.

Henry VIII's Acts of Union of 1536 and 1542/3, which united England and Wales, abolished the Marcher lordships and removed the independence they had enjoyed.

Arthur Gilbertson, incoming Sheriff of the County of Glamorgan; County Alderman E. Gwynfryn Davies, Chairman of Glamorgan County Council; John Traherne, outgoing Sheriff; Sir Cennydd Traherne, Lord-Lieutenant of the County of Glamorgan. Photographed in County Hall after the inauguration ceremony, 1970.

Wales was divided into shires on the model of English counties, and county administration was introduced on the English pattern, based locally on the support and activities of justices of the peace. The office of sheriff was retained, to become an annual appointment.

Following the Acts of Union the gentry families of Wales benefited from more settled times and from the greater prosperity which followed. Eagerly they grasped the opportunities offered by public office, and the advantages which this conferred in status and local power. They served as justices of the peace locally, and they provided members of Parliament in London. The list of Glamorgan sheriffs of the sixteenth and seventeenth centuries is dominated by the names of the leading gentry families, Herbert, Mansel, Carne, Bassett, Mathew, Stradling, Turbervill, Lewis, Kemeys and others, as succeeding generations and different branches of these families held office. Some men served on more than one occasion, including Edward Kemeys of Cefn Mably, sheriff on four separate occasions between 1575 and 1605, despite, after the first three terms, detention in the Fleet prison and a heavy fine for abusing his shrieval office.

During the succeeding two centuries the involvement of Glamorgan's landowning families in the shrievalty widened to include a growing number of

Martin Thomas, incoming Sheriff of the County of West Glamorgan, Claud Gerald Bellingham, outgoing Sheriff, and trumpeters, 1976.

lesser gentry families whose wealth was derived from fewer acres. They were not deterred from holding office despite the considerable expenditure it entailed and the reduced opportunities available for direct influence and personal gain, aspects which had made the office desirable in earlier centuries.

Many of the sheriff's duties were related to the courts of justice. The major court in the county was that of Quarter Sessions. This brought justices of the peace together four times a year, both to transact the business of the county and to deal with those accused of offences against the law. It was the sheriff who was responsible for the 'bodies' of the prisoners in the county gaol, those awaiting trial or, after sentence, awaiting their dispatch to the gallows or to a port of embarkation for transportation overseas. If the guilty were to swing, it was the sheriff and his men who oversaw the execution, and ate a hearty breakfast afterwards.

The precept to cause the Sessions to be held was addressed to the sheriff. The day-to-day work, however – the issue of writs and the enforcement of court orders – was carried out on his behalf by his under sheriff, an attorney by profession who

Lieutenant-Colonel David Cox, incoming Sheriff of the County of Mid Glamorgan, Islwyn Rees, outgoing Sheriff, and police trumpeters outside County Hall, 1991.

in time enjoyed a greater continuity of office if reappointed to serve by successive sheriffs.

Above the Court of Quarter Sessions was the Court of Great Sessions, the precursor of the later Assizes in Wales, held twice a year. It was the sheriff who received the Great Sessions judge into the county, meeting him in his coach at the county boundary. The sheriff escorted the judge in procession to court and to church, the sheriff's chaplain, his trumpeters and his javelin men adding to the ceremonial. The sheriff was responsible for overseeing the judge's lodging and providing his entertainment. He was also expected to provide dinners and drink for a large number of friends, acquaintances, holders of public office and an assortment of followers.

As returning officer the sheriff had the duty of announcing the result of a contested parliamentary election. An eighteenth-century poll lasted for several days, and the ballot was an open one, each vote marked in the poll book for all to see. Even so, the integrity of a sheriff might still be in doubt. In 1744, when the Kemeys of the day stood as a parliamentary candidate, Lord Mansel of Margam warned him to keep an eye on the sheriff, and to force the declaration to be made before the sheriff left the stand.

The Reverend Chancellor James Keane, Sheriff's Chaplain; Alastair Golley, incoming Sheriff of the County of South Glamorgan; Captain Norman Lloyd-Edwards RNR, Lord-Lieutenant of the County of South Glamorgan; Michael Clay, outgoing Sheriff; John Otto-Jones, Under Sheriff. Photographed after the inauguration ceremony, 1992.

From the middle of the eighteenth century the predominance of landowning families deriving their status and wealth from their estates began to change as industrial development affected the area's economy and society. First copper works in the west, then iron works in the north of Glamorgan attracted the entrepreneurial qualities and expertise of men drawn almost entirely from outside the county. By the early nineteenth century these new families had built up their positions, and in their turn had acquired land and sufficient local status for the names Bacon, Guest, Tait, Crawshay, Hill, Homfray, Vivian and Morris to appear in the shrieval lists beside those of long-established county families.

By the end of the nineteenth century and the first half of the twentieth century, even greater industrial expansion, linked with the building of docks and railways, had brought into the shrievalty numerous representatives from the coal, iron and steel, and manufacturing industries, as well as from ship-owning and coal-exporting businesses. Land was no longer the best investment for capital. The period which saw the rise in importance of industry and commerce also witnessed the decline of many landowning families. Economic developments elsewhere in the world led to agricultural depression in Britain with the loss of revenue from rents; this forced the sale and fragmentation of many estates, unless mineral resources

In the centre Mrs Kathrin Thomas, Sheriff of the County of Mid Glamorgan, flanked by the Sheriffs of Dyfed and Gwent. On the left Eden Hughes Evans, Sheriff of the County of West Glamorgan, on the right Sir Brooke Boothby, Sheriff of the County of South Glamorgan. The group is framed by javelin men provided by the police authority. Photographed in October 1986 outside the Prebendal House, Llandaff, on the occasion of the annual Service for those concerned with the Administration of Justice. This service is held in two years out of three at Llandaff Cathedral; in the third year it takes place in St Mary's, Swansea.

below the soil had brought new wealth. The introduction of inheritance taxes in 1894 further weakened the position of gentry families, and they were to suffer tragic losses in the First World War from the slaughter of their sons.

The long-established landowning families of the area had provided sheriffs for the county through the centuries, and were often linked with each other by marriage. These families and their relationships were explored in a volume on the

HM The Queen at Margam Orangery, 1988. Sir Michael Llewellyn, Lord-Lieutenant of the County of West Glamorgan, presents Mr Peter Scott, DL. Also in the photograph: the Chairman of West Glamorgan County Council, County Councillor D. T. Vernon Davies, and the Clerk to West Glamorgan County Council, Mr Michael Rush.

sheriffs who had held office in Glamorgan between 1541 and 1966, a book published by Mr George Williams of Llanharan House to mark his shrieval year.

This present volume brings that list up to date and documents the sheriffs who have held office in the county of Glamorgan since 1966, and in the three counties of Glamorgan since 1974. It offers an opportunity to analyse the very different composition of the recent shrievalty. The short biographical notes on individual sheriffs which follow can give only selected summaries of the wealth of experience, activity and achievements offered by these prominent members of the community.

The office continues to be an almost entirely male preserve. In Glamorgan, four women only have served (Glamorgan 1968, Mid Glamorgan 1986 and 1993, and South Glamorgan 1994). Most of the sheriffs, however, have had the support of their wives, who have accompanied their husbands on many occasions, and taken charge of the not inconsiderable arrangements for entertaining.

Families who provided sheriffs in past centuries are still represented by sheriffs in the modern list. Several can point to ancestors who served in the sixteenth, seventeenth and eighteenth centuries. They have long-established associations with the county as landowners, but representation now comes as well from those who

HM The Queen arrives at Treherbert, Mid Glamorgan, to open the Glenrhondda Court Development and visit one of the tenants' flats, 1989. The Lord-Lieutenant, Mr Douglas Badham, presents the Sheriff, Mr John Tamplin, and Mrs Tamplin. The Vice Lord-Lieutenant, Mr George Williams, escorts HRH The Duke of Edinburgh. Also in the picture are the Chairman of Mid Glamorgan County Council, County Councillor Tom O'Brien, and Mrs O'Brien, and the Chief Executive to Mid Glamorgan County Council, Mr D. Hugh Thomas, and Mrs Thomas.

farmed land as freeholders or as tenant farmers; their genealogy, though of equal antiquity, may not have been fully recorded or yet researched. Some sheriffs can point to the precise year in the nineteenth century when their forebears arrived in south Wales, attracted into a developing industrial area where there were opportunities to provide new services. A number founded firms which continue today and in which their grandchildren play an active part. Other recent sheriffs, by contrast, are the first of their line to settle in Glamorgan, brought to the area by their careers in industry or commerce.

During the period since 1966 there has been one example of a father and son serving in the office (Glamorgan 1966 and Mid Glamorgan 1985); appropriately they continue a tradition within a family which found a sheriff for the county as early as 1566. Possibly a unique situation is that of three brothers who have served as sheriffs in Glamorgan (1972), South Glamorgan (1978), and Pembrokeshire (1963).

During the period since 1966 about half the sheriffs have had Welsh surnames, with roots in Glamorgan or in neighbouring Welsh counties. The English, Scottish and Irish names came into the area mainly in the nineteenth and twentieth

HRH The Prince of Wales arrives at Cardiff–Wales Airport, 1993. The Lord-Lieutenant of the County of South Glamorgan, Captain Norman Lloyd-Edwards, RNR, presents the Sheriff, Commander John Curteis, and Mrs Curteis, and the Chairman of South Glamorgan County Council, County Councillor Douglas Francies.

centuries. One sheriff had a Swedish father who settled in Cardiff, and the grandfather of another came from Italy. One, though of Welsh ancestry, was born and brought up in Canada, and retains his Canadian citizenship.

English public schools have educated a number of Glamorgan sheriffs. Many are the products of grammar schools of excellence. One records that he had sampled seventeen different educational establishments before he settled into his secondary school. Oxford, Cambridge, the London School of Economics, redbrick universities, medical schools, technical colleges and colleges of further education, as well as Sandhurst, all have shaped future sheriffs. One sheriff spent time at the Massachusetts Institute of Technology and at Harvard, another at the Sorbonne.

Many saw war service in the army, navy or air force. They participated during the Second World War in Africa, the Middle and Far East, in the Salerno landing and the Italian campaign, in the Normandy landings and in Europe. Many have remained active in the reserve forces. One was captured in 1942 at Singapore and as a prisoner of war was forced to work on the Singapore–Bangkok railway. One, when called up, was drafted into the coal-mines as a 'Bevin Boy', and worked underground at Lewis Merthyr Colliery. Another spent part of his childhood on the other side of the Atlantic, a wartime evacuee to the USA.

In the nineteenth and early twentieth centuries many sheriffs were associated

The Hon. Mr Justice Garland being shown the Llanwern Steel Works by its director, Bill Harrison, 1987. The accompanying party, in hard hats and goggles, consists of Peter Allen, the Sheriff who arranged the visit, and Mrs Allen, Edward Rea, the former Sheriff, and Mrs Rea, the Under Sheriff, John Otto-Jones, and Mrs Otto-Jones, Mrs Margaret Cooper, Clerk to Mr Justice Garland, and Mrs Harrison.

with the traditional heavy industries of south Wales – iron and steel, and the production and export of coal. In recent years these traditional industries have been transformed, as countrywide rationalization of resources has led to reorganization and reduction; some Glamorgan sheriffs have been closely involved in these changes during their careers in industry. Activity in engineering continues, and several sheriffs have spent their working lives developing a diversity of light industries within the area. South Wales docks no longer export coal to a world market, but one sheriff exports building materials and sanitary ware to developing countries; others are involved with retailing locally and across Britain. Recent shrieval lists have included a growing number of members of the professions: medical men, architects and chartered surveyors, bankers and accountants. Among the service industries, baking and brewing are represented, as well as the production of Welsh wine from a Mid Glamorgan vineyard. The success of one sheriff in the catering industry reaches beyond Wales and the promotion of Welsh products to the provision of millions of school meals to pupils in Saudi Arabia.

In the course of their careers some have worked abroad, in West Africa, the Middle East and the USA, or wherever their military careers have required. Some have used their talents for administration, others have shared their academic

The Sheriff of the County of South Glamorgan, Commander John Curteis, meets The Hon. Mr Justice Kirkwood (High Court Judge) upon his arrival at the Judge's Lodgings, Radyr, Cardiff. John Curteis and Andrew Kirkwood were schoolboys in the same house at Radley College, overlapping by two years.

Sergeant Peter William Hall, Swansea, recipient of the Shrieval Cup, 1991, after its presentation by the Sheriff of the County of West Glamorgan.

knowledge as visiting professors abroad. Many have associations with the University of Wales, and with its constituent colleges, serving as Court or Council members. On a local level they act as school governors. Some sit on the Governing Body of the Church in Wales, or find time to serve as churchwardens in their parish churches or elders in their Nonconformist chapels. Some have been associated with training schemes for the unemployed, and with improving facilities for the handicapped. Many are active in the Priory for Wales of the Most Venerable Order of the Hospital of St John of Jerusalem and ex-servicemen's associations, and a wide range of charitable organizations benefit from their support. One arranges pilgrimages each year to Lourdes.

Many in their younger days have been active in sport, playing rugby, cricket, tennis and squash. Their interest continues as spectators and as patrons of local clubs, but at least one has extended his time on the field as a rugby referee. One has water-skied, another played squash for Wales. Golf attracts many; some take their game seriously, others resolutely do not. An interest in vintage cars involved one in car restoration and the Brighton Run, while another was co-driver of a 1925 3-litre Bentley on a 2,000-mile journey through South Africa; yet another raced Bugattis.

One sheriff was chairman of the Welsh Arts Council. Several collect antiques, porcelain or modern art, but few actually paint. One has had a life-long fascination with cinematography. Many attend music concerts and opera, and give their support to national and local companies and festivals. A few admit to playing the piano, another is an organist who delights his friends and acquaintances with his playing. One is a bell-ringer. Amateur operatics have enlisted the voices of two or three, likewise local amateur dramatics.

Many of the sheriffs have served in the community as justices of the peace, several act as deputy lieutenants, and some have been appointed to the lieutenancy of their county, becoming the sovereign's representative. In contrast with the yearly office of shrievalty this is a continuing duty, undertaken until retirement.

The office of sheriff might well have been extinguished in the early 1970s in the course of the reorganization of courts of law and the replacement of Assizes and Quarter Sessions by Crown Courts. It was suggested that the office of sheriff had lost virtually all its executive power and could be dispensed with. The shrievalty was, however, after strong representations, retained, and it was at this time that the Shrievalty Association of Great Britain was brought into being, the late Arthur Gilbertson of Glamorgan playing a large part in its formation.

It was also Arthur Gilbertson who, in 1982, persuaded those who had served as sheriff within Glamorgan to fund the provision of the Shrieval Cup, to be awarded annually for outstanding police service to the community. The presentation is made each year by the sheriff appropriate to the area of Glamorgan from which the police officer recipient comes.

Many of the more irksome duties attendant upon the office have dwindled and the abolition of capital punishment (except in cases of treason) removes the need for the sheriff's presence at an execution, and his chaplain's 'Amen' when a death sentence was passed. The sheriff continues to attend upon each High Court judge's first working day at the relevant Crown Court. The sheriff for West Glamorgan attends at Swansea, and the sheriff for South Glamorgan at Cardiff (where there is a special high sheriff's room for his, or her, accommodation). The sheriff for Mid Glamorgan is in attendance on the rarer occasions when the Crown Court brings a High Court judge to Merthyr Tydfil, but also attends upon the judges at both Cardiff and Swansea. With regard to the enforcement of writs, and the payment of rewards, this is now the responsibility of the under sheriff, acting in the name of the sheriff.

The tradition of the reception and entertainment of judges is continued in luncheons and dinner parties which also offer an opportunity to recognize by association those who have been active in public service and voluntary organizations. The sheriff is required to be in attendance during the visits of royalty. Second only to the lord-lieutenant in matters of precedence (or deferring out of courtesy to a lord mayor or mayor in a borough), the sheriff adds the dignity of his or her office to ceremonial occasions. His or her presence as a prestigious guest is sought by many organizations, and the sheriff, in the last decade of the twentieth century, still plays a significant role in county affairs and in county society.

Biographical Notes on Glamorgan Sheriffs
since 1966
and
on the Sheriffs of the Counties of
Mid Glamorgan, South Glamorgan and
West Glamorgan 1974–1993

GEORGE MERVYN WILLIAMS

CBE, MC, CStJ, TD, JP, DL 1967–86. HM Vice Lord-Lieutenant of the county of Mid Glamorgan 1986–93.

Born: 1918, London.
Educated: Radley College.
Married: Grizel Margaretta Cochrane Stewart, DStJ, one son (HS Mid Glamorgan 1985).

Commissioned in Royal Fusiliers (TA) 1938. Served in 1939–45 war in North Africa, Italy, Iraq, Iran and Greece, retiring as major. Worked for Great Universal Stores 1946–49, and for Christie-Tyler PLC 1949–85, its chairman 1959–85. A former director of Lloyds Bank, and chairman of its South Wales Region 1977–87.

Recreations: gardening – he has created a notable garden at Craig y Bwla, his Crickhowell home.

Grandson of Morgan Stuart Williams of Aberpergwm and St Donat's Castle (HS 1875), great-grandson of William Williams (HS 1830), and descended from William ap Jenkin of Aberpergwm (HS 1566). A member of a landowning and coal-owning family who turned to manufacturing in an industry new to the county which, by 1985, was employing over 3,000 people.

JIM STANLEY HAMILTON MATHEWS

Born: 1921, Southsea, Hants.
Educated: Shrewsbury School.
Married: Wendy Venables, two sons, one daughter.

Enlisted in Royal Air Force in 1941 as a pilot. Served in North Africa, flying Wellingtons on anti-submarine patrols and naval co-operation. In 1946 joined father in the management of old-established property companies, based in Cardiff. In 1988, following the sale of the Cardiff Exchange building, and the Cardiff High Street and Duke Street Arcades, moved his office to Monmouth.

Recreations: life and living.

Family associations with Glamorgan go back to 1860.

Mrs SUSAN EVA WILLIAMS

MBE, DStJ, JP 1961–85, DL 1974–81, HM Lieutenant for the county of South Glamorgan 1981–85, HM Lord-Lieutenant for the county of South Glamorgan 1985–89

Born: 1915, Llantwit Major.
Educated: St James, West Malvern.
Married: 1950, Charles Crofts Llewellyn Williams, MC, DL, JP (died 1952).

Served in the Women's Auxiliary Air Force 1939–45, retiring as wing officer. In 1958 was made an MBE for her work in connection with the Cardiff Empire Commonwealth Games, when she was in charge of all the women athletes. The first woman to be appointed High Sheriff of Glamorgan, and the first woman to be appointed a Lord-Lieutenant in Wales. A Liveryman of the Welsh Livery Guild.

Recreations: National Hunt Racing. Most successful horse owned was Tree Tangle in seasons 1972–76.

Great-granddaughter of Charles Crofts Williams of Roath Court who was four times mayor of Cardiff (HS 1859), and granddaughter of Charles Henry Williams (HS 1872).

JOHN RHODRI LLEWELLYN TRAHERNE
KStJ, DL

Born: 1913, Coedarhydyglyn.
Died: 1987.
Educated: Clifton College; RMC Sandhurst.
Married: Lesley Molly Odham, two daughters, one son.

Commissioned in The Welch Regiment in 1933. War service in Africa, Burma and Cyprus. Mentioned in dispatches three times. After the war served in Africa, Britain, Germany and in Cyprus during the emergency. Lieutenant-colonel 1956. Commanded the 1st Battalion, The Welch Regiment. Principal secretary of the Priory for Wales of the Most Venerable Order of the Hospital of St John of Jerusalem and chief commissioner for Wales of St John's Ambulance Brigade 1966–76.

The Traherne family were of Castellau, Llantrisant, by the end of the sixteenth century (HS 1801, 1812, 1863). Lieutenant-Colonel J. R. Ll. Traherne returned with his family to Castellau in 1960, retiring to Leominster in 1976. Sir Cennydd Traherne, KG, of Coedarhydyglyn, brother of the sheriff, was HM Lord-Lieutenant of Glamorgan and of the Three Counties of Glamorgan 1952–85.

ARTHUR GEOFFREY GILBERTSON

CStJ, JP

Born: 1913, Gellygron, Pontardawe.
Died: 1991.
Educated: Shrewsbury School.
Married: Hilarie Annette Williams-Thomas, three daughters.

After an early business career in W. Gilbertson & Co. Ltd, steel, tinplate and galvanized steel manufacturers of Pontardawe, and with Richard Thomas & Baldwins Ltd, as well as two years in America working in steel strip mills in Youngstown, Ohio, and Chicago, he joined Brown Lenox & Co. Ltd of Pontypridd in 1949, becoming managing director at Pontypridd and company chairman at Millwall. Honorary lay secretary of the Llandaff Diocesan Conference, past member of the Governing Body and of the Representative Body of the Church in Wales. Member of the Court of Governors of the University College of South Wales and Monmouthshire.

Grandson of Arthur Gilbertson of Pontardawe (HS 1892) and of Joseph Moore Gwyn (HS Breconshire 1902). Great-grandson of Howell Gwyn (HS Glamorgan 1837, Carmarthenshire 1838 and Breconshire 1844) and descended from Howell Gwyn (HS Breconshire 1761).

After his year in office he sought support from all previous sheriffs to fund the 'Shrievalty Cup' which is presented annually for outstanding police service to the community in Glamorgan. Together with Jeremy Elwes (HS Lincolnshire) and Sir Tom Burgess (HS Cumberland), he founded the 'Shrievalty Association'.

CHRISTOPHER METHUEN-CAMPBELL

Born: 1928, Renfrew, Scotland.
Educated: Eton; Magdalen College,
Cambridge.
Married: 1. Oona Treherne, one
son, three daughters.
2. Judith Crowther, one son.

National service with the Scots Guards.

Gentleman, with interests in farming, conservation and estate management. Active in Gower peninsular organizations, including community council and Lifeboat Crew Committee.

Recreations: sailing and cruising off the South Coast and France. Photography and gardening. Italian art and architecture.

Great-great-grandson of Christopher Rice Mansel Talbot of Margam and Penrice, MP 1830–90 and HM Lord-Lieutenant of Glamorgan. The Mansel and Mansel Talbot families have provided sheriffs to the county on fifteen occasions since the sixteenth century, commencing with Sir Rice Mansel in 1542.

GEORGE FORBES RAYMOND HAYES

CStJ, MA(Cantab.), CEng, FIMechE, FRHS, FRAS, Fellow of University of Wales College of Cardiff

Born: 1917, Porthcawl.
Educated: Wycliffe College, Stonehouse; Trinity College, Cambridge.
Married: Jean Cory, one son, one daughter.

Commissioned in 81 Field Regiment, Royal Artillery (TA) 1938–39. Served in REME 1943–46 on Lines of Communication Troops Workshop in the Normandy landing; later attached to 21 Army Group HQ. Responsible for valuation and disposal of British assets in Normandy to the French and Belgian governments.

Career spent in engineering. Director and chairman of Sheppard & Sons (later Hayes Industries) 1946–66. Director of Hill Samuel & Co. Ltd 1966–76, and chairman of Henley Forklift 1973–75. Founder chairman of CBI Council, Wales, 1965. Member of the Court of the Worshipful Company of Tin Plate Workers alias Wire Workers (Master 1975–76). Freeman of the City of London and member of the Court of the Welsh Livery Guild.

Recreations: plays a Walker pipe organ in the hall at Brocastle and enjoys using his house for musical entertainments; gardening, golf and travel.

Brother to Richard Hayes (HS Pembrokeshire 1963) and Francis Hayes (HS South Glamorgan 1978).

MATHEW CARADOC THOMAS PRICHARD

CBE, BA, DL

Born: 1943, Cheshire (where his father was stationed in wartime).
Educated: Eton; New College, Oxford.
Married: Angela Maples, one son, two daughters.

In the 1960s worked in the educational and marketing departments of Penguin Books. The grandson of Agatha Christie, since 1970 the chairman of Agatha Christie Ltd, the company which owns and manages her literary copyrights and television and film rights. Since 1985 chairman of Booker Entertainment which deals with James Bond, Georgette Heyer and other literary and entertainment properties. In 1980 became a member of the Welsh Arts Council, and its chairman 1986–94. Vice-president of the National Museum of Wales, and chairman of the Cardiff Bay Opera House Trust.

Recreations: collects modern British pictures, ceramics and glass, and is a keen opera-goer. Plays golf, watches cricket, walks dogs and is devoted to family life at Pwllywrach.

Descended from the Thomas family of Treoes/Tregroes (HS 1551, 1772, 1777).

JOHN LEWIS MAYBERY BEVAN

MA (Cantab.), FIMechE, TD, DL

Born: 1919, Neath.
Educated: Stowe; Gonville and Caius College, Cambridge.
Married: Barbara Elizabeth Ware (died 1991), three sons.

War service 1939–45, with the Territorial Army 132 (W) Field Regiment, Royal Artillery, in the Middle East, Sicily, Italy and Austria. Awarded American Bronze Star. Twice wounded.

A career in the steel industry 1947–73. Director of Briton Ferry Steel Co. Ltd, Baglan Engineering Co., Llanelli Steel Company and general manager of Steel Company of Wales, ORB Works, Newport. In 1975–76 planted Croffta Vineyard, at Groesfaen, Pontyclun, for the commercial production of Welsh wine, using Müller-Thurgau, Seyval Blanc and Madeleine-Angevine grape varieties.

Recreations: sailing and fishing.

Son of Colonel John Maybery Bevan, MC (HS 1929 Carmarthenshire). The family roots lie in the Kidwelly area of Carmarthenshire.

Sir **LESLIE JOSEPH**
Knight Bachelor, DL

Born: 1908, Swansea.
Died: 1992.
Educated: The King's
School, Canterbury;
Swansea Technical College.
Married: 1. Emily Murphy
(died 1987), two daughters.
2. Christine Jones.

Military service in Sudan as major in Royal Engineers 1940–46.

Career in mechanical engineering and in the entertainment industry, managing director of Coney Beach, Porthcawl, and of the Festival Gardens, Battersea Park, London. Chairman of Trusthouse Forte Leisure. Member of the Arts Committee of the National Museum of Wales, and of the Royal Society of Arts. Council member, University College of Swansea.

Recreations: collecting porcelain, medals, paintings of old Swansea, mainly shipping. Co-author of *Swansea Porcelain* (1988).

Family was originally from Carmarthenshire, but has had a long association with Glamorgan.

DOUGLAS GEORGE BADHAM

CBE, KStJ, JP, FCA
HM Lieutenant for the county of Mid Glamorgan 1982–85, HM Lord-Lieutenant
for the county of Mid Glamorgan 1985–89

Born: 1914, Aberdare.
Educated: Leys School, Cambridge.
Married: Doreen Spencer Phillips, two
daughters.

Chartered accountant, executive director of Powell Duffryn Group 1938–69. Served
as chairman of the South Wales Regional Advisory Committee of the Forestry
Commission, the Development Corporation for Wales, the National Health
Service Staff Commission, the Industry and Planning Panel of the Welsh Council
and of the Economic Forestry Group; deputy chairman of the Welsh Development
Agency. Member of University of Wales Institute of Science and Technology
Council, of the British Gas Corporation and of the Wales and the Marches
Telecommunications Board.

Recreations: forestry.

His forebears, paternal from Pembrokeshire and maternal from north Wales,
arrived in the Cynon Valley in about 1870.

DOUGLAS ANDREW SCOTT

OBE, JP, FCIOB

Born: 1920, Port Talbot.
Educated: Port Talbot County School;
Loughborough College.
Married: Renne Olive Morgan, two sons, two
daughters.

Joined Senior OTC (Sherwood Foresters) 1938. Commissioned in Royal Engineers 1940. Fought with 46th Infantry Division in North Africa and Italy. Commanded minefield breaching parties on Red Beach at H.Hour on D-Day at Salerno landings in September 1943. Wounded by exploding mine and again in battle to capture Naples. Instructor, School of Military Engineering, Egypt. Attached Royal Navy for capture of Athens and worked with SBS in Greece. Instructor, School of Military Engineering, Ripon, UK. Commanded 283 Field Squadron RE (TA) 1952–55.

In 1945 became managing director of Andrew Scott (Civil Engineers) Ltd, the third generation in the family business of civil engineering contractors, the largest indigenous firm in Wales. Chairman of Andrew Scott Holdings Ltd and all other companies in the group from 1966 till retirement in 1982 when he was appointed president. Member of Federation of Civil Engineering Contractors South Wales Section and on Executive Committee 1950–85. Chairman 1953, 1963, 1964, member of its national Council 1952–55, 1962–66.

Member of Regional Joint Advisory Committee for Wales, Ministry of Works 1964–79. Awarded Queen's Jubilee Medal 1977. Member of the CBI Council for Wales 1967–77 and of the CBI Regional Development Committee. Member of three successive Welsh Councils 1968–79, chairman of Communications Panel 1974–79. Founder president of South Wales Construction Accident Prevention Group 1971–89. Founder president of RNLI Lifeboat Station Port Talbot, 1966 to date, life governor of RNLI. President of Aberavon Conservative and Unionist Association 1969–74 and of Port Talbot and District Scout Association 1971. Regional leader for Wales of the Emergency Construction Organization (Civil Defence) 1965.

Recreations: sailing, travel, vintage cars, coastal walking and enjoying the company of grandchildren.

Grandson of Thomas Scott who founded the family firm in Lanarkshire in the mid-nineteenth century and established its south Wales branch in the 1890s. A fourth generation, Peter Scott DL, is the present chairman. Grandson of Henry Walsh, a local builders' merchant, JP, mayor of Aberavon 1891–92 and 1907–08.

MURRAY ADAMS McLAGGAN

MA (Oxon.), JP, HM Lord-Lieutenant for the county of Mid Glamorgan, appointed 1990

Born: 1929, London.
Educated: Winchester College; New College, Oxford.
Married: Jennifer Nicholl (eldest daughter of Robert Iltyd Nicholl of Merthyr Mawr), two sons, one daughter.

Second lieutenant, Royal Artillery, serving in Hong Kong 1948–50.

Called to the Bar 1955, Lincoln's Inn, London, student and tutor in law at Christ Church, Oxford, 1957–66. Career in farming and estate management. Past chairman of the Glamorgan Naturalists' Trust, the Timber Growers' Association (South Wales), the Historic Houses Association (Wales). Chairman of the Forestry Commission Regional Advisory Committee (Wales Conservancy), the National Rivers Authority (Wales), the Regional Flood Defence Committee, and past chairman of the National Trust Committee for Wales. Past member of the South Wales Police Authority. Member of the National Rivers Authority, the Wales Regional Advisory Board and the Parliamentary Boundary Commission for Wales.

Recreations: antiquarian books, amateur dramatics, dendrology, landscape garden design and conservation.

Son of Sir John Douglas McLaggan, KCVO, FRCS, formerly aurist to King George VI, Queen Mary and Queen Elizabeth II.

GEORGE MORGAN THOMAS LINDSAY

DL

Born: 1918, Dublin.
Died: 1990.
Educated: Wellington; Royal Military Academy, Woolwich.
Married: Jennifer Mary Ferry, two sons.

Commissioned in Royal Artillery 1938, war service in Gibraltar, Malta, north-west Europe. Mentioned in dispatches. Passed Staff College 1950, served in Australia, Germany, and Canada. Retired from the army in 1963 to farm 1,200 acres in Llanbradach and Llantrithyd.

Chairman and president of the Conservative Association, Salisbury constituency 1971–78, and president of the Conservative Association, Bridgend constituency 1983–90. Chairman and president of the Glamorgan Executive Committee of the Country Landowners Association. Chairman of the Country Landowners Association Welsh Water Committee 1986–89. Vice-chairman of the South Wales Board of the Prince's Youth Business Trust. Member of the Prince's Trust Committee 1983–90.

Recreations: country pursuits and interest in history.

Descended on the distaff side from the Thomas family of Llanbradach, who provided the county with sheriffs in 1675, 1705, 1728 and 1870.

ROBERT WATKIN STACEY KNIGHT
DL, FRICS

Born: 1937, Hereford.
Educated: Radley College.
Married: Susan Mary Ball, two sons, one daughter.

The sheriff photographed with his father, HM Lieutenant for the County of Mid Glamorgan.

National service 1956–58, commissioned in the Welsh Guards.

A chartered surveyor, senior partner of Cooke and Arkwright. Director of various property companies. Also a farming partner in 1,200-acre family dairy and arable enterprise at Tythegston. Board member of the Land Authority for Wales and governor of the Cardiff Institute for Higher Education. Member of the Royal Agricultural Society of England and the Royal Horticultural Society. President of the Welsh Guards Association, Mid Glamorgan. Chairman of the Glamorgan and Gwent Branch of the Country Landowners Association and council member.

Recreations: gardening, shooting and tennis.

Son of Henry Lougher Knight, HM Lieutenant for the county of Mid Glamorgan 1974–82. The Knight family furnished sheriffs in 1737 and 1794, and their Lougher forebears of Tythegston and Nottage in 1635, 1656 and 1696.

EDWARD ARTHUR LEWIS

CStJ, BA (Wales), JP, DL

Born: 1915, Pontypridd.
Died: 1992.
Educated: Pontypridd Boys' Grammar School; University College of South Wales and Monmouthshire, Cardiff; Jesus College, Oxford.
Married: Mrs Nancy Llewellyn (née Williams), one son, two daughters.

Served in the Colonial Administrative Service, Nigeria 1939–55, including assignment to the Foreign Office for service in the Spanish Territories of the Gulf of Guinea and the Gaboon, French Equatorial Africa 1946–49. Retired in 1955 as permanent secretary, Ministry of Public Health, Ibadan. Secretary to the South-Western Division of the National Coal Board 1955–72. General commissioner of taxes 1971–85, housing commissioner 1972–74.

Member of numerous statutory bodies, including the Welsh Industrial Estates Corporation, Wales and the Marches Postal Board, the Immigration Appeal Tribunal (London), the VAT Tribunal (Cardiff), the Welsh Joint Education Committee, the Glamorgan River Authority, the Mental Health Service Tribunal for Wales, Mid Glamorgan Health Authority, Glamorgan/Mid Glamorgan Local Education Authority. Chairman of the Civil Service Commission Appointments Board. Assessor under the Race Relations Act. Member of the Court of Governors of University College, Cardiff, and president of the Students' Union Council. Elected fellow of University College, Cardiff, 1985. Trustee of the Rhondda Baptist Chapel, Pontypridd.

Recreations: an active sportsman in his student days. Honorary secretary and chairman of the Cardiff and District Outward Bound Association.

Members of the family were active as mining engineers in nineteenth-century Glamorgan, but the family's eighteenth-century roots lay in Cardiganshire.

WILLIAM KINGDON EYNON

Born: 1936, Swansea.
Educated: Harrow; Royal Agricultural College of Cirencester.
Married: Christine Joseph (daughter of Sir Leslie Joseph, HS Mid 1975), three daughters, three sons.

Chairman and managing director of Eynons Ltd, a family baking business founded in Swansea in the last century.

Recreations: has water-skied for Wales and played squash for Glamorgan. Enjoys golf, snow-skiing, tennis and boating. Involved with charities and environmental concerns. The patron of the Cwm Disability Centre for Independent Living at the Cwm Cheshire Home and an enthusiastic supporter of Friends of the Earth Cymru, based at Porthcawl.

Eynons have been in Gower since the eleventh century. A number of recent forebears are buried in Penrice churchyard.

ALAN EDWARD MAYER

DL, KSG

Born: 1939, Leamington Spa, War.
Educated: Ampleforth College, York.
Married: Anna Rickaby, three sons.

In 1956 joined his maternal grandfather's family business, Edward Curran Engineering Ltd, Cardiff. Appointed director of Curran Oils Ltd, Cardiff, in 1963, and left Edward Curran in 1975, after Reed International take-over, to found his own company, Alan Mayer Export Ltd, based in Pontypridd, and operating in the Caribbean, Africa and the Far East. Specializes in building materials and hardware. Chairman of the South Wales Exporters' Club and a council member of the British Exporters' Association. Freeman of the City of London and Liveryman of the Worshipful Company of Glaziers and Painters of Glass. Active member of All Hallows Church, Llantrisant. Has had a life-long interest in taking sick or handicapped people to Lourdes and has arranged yearly visits since 1957. Created a Knight of St Gregory in 1984.

Recreations: enjoys shooting, fishing, sailing, golf and painting.

His maternal grandfather was one of the Irish who put down roots in Cardiff: his paternal grandfather originated in Bavaria.

EDWARD REA

OBE, FBIM, FInstD, DL

Born: 1930, Blaenau Ffestiniog, Merioneth.
Educated: Ffestiniog Grammar School.
Married: Martha Ellen Jones, two sons, one daughter (including twins).

National service in Royal Signals 1953–55. Active with reserve forces, TAVRA.

Founded Wella Company, manufacturing toiletries and cosmetics, managing director of Ondawel (GB) Ltd in Pontyclun, subsequently chairman of D. G. Durham Richards Ltd, insurance brokers. Chairman of the Institute of Directors, Wales, and of the South Wales Electricity Board. Member of the Development Board for Rural Wales, and of the Finance Committee of the Royal National Eisteddfod. A governor of Howell's School, Llandaff, and of the Wales Equality Centre.

Recreations: shooting, reading and computing.

His grandfather came to Britain from Italy; on the distaff side his forebears are Welsh.

OWAIN ANTHONY MERVYN WILLIAMS

OStJ, DL

Born: 1955, Llanharan.
Educated: Eton.
Married: Bethan Mary Watkins, two daughters.

After voluntary service as a teacher in Kenya, became negotiator for Knight, Frank and Rutley, chartered surveyors, London. Since 1980 has been concerned with the management of woodlands at Llanharan and the Cwrt-yr-Ala Estate, and has developed commercial activities at Llanharan House. Director of Williams and Morgan Ltd and occupied with various building and property interests. President of the Bridgend Show Society, member of the St John Council for Mid Glamorgan and vice-chancellor of the Most Venerable Order of the Hospital of St John of Jerusalem Priory for Wales. Foundation governor of St Michael's Roman Catholic School, Treforest.

Recreations: walking, forestry, travel and politics.

Son of George Williams (HS 1966), q.v.

Mrs KATHRIN ELIZABETH THOMAS

JP, DL 1989–93, HM Vice Lord-Lieutenant for the county of **Mid Glamorgan** from 1993

Born: 1944, Radyr.
Educated: Cheltenham Ladies' College; the Sorbonne.
Married: Edward Vaughan Thomas, two sons.

From her marriage in 1967 her career has been that of a family company director, farmer's wife, and mother. A deputy president of the Mid Glamorgan branch of the British Red Cross Society, member of the Mid Glamorgan War Pensions Committee, the Barnardo's Centenary Appeal, the South Wales Committee of the Prince's Trust, the Prince of Wales' Committee, current chairman of the Mid Glamorgan Family Health Services Authority, trustee of the Civic Trust for Wales and of Llandovery College.

Recreations: reading, milking and tractor-driving.

Her father, Dillwyn Evans, an orthopaedic surgeon, came from a family which had farmed for generations in the Vale of Glamorgan; numbered among her ancestors is William Edwards, the builder of the renowned Pontypridd bridge.

PETER DOBSON ALLEN
CBE, BSc, CEng, FIM, DL

Born: 1931, Dewsbury, Yorks.
Educated: Wheelwright Grammar School,
Dewsbury; Rotherham College of
Technology; Birmingham University.
Married: Janet Thurman, three sons.

National service 1955–57, commissioned in the Royal Artillery.

Between 1957 and 1972 held managerial appointments within the United Steel Companies and in British Steel in Yorkshire and in the Midlands. Moved to Wales in 1972 as director, Port Talbot Works, and in 1976 was appointed managing director, Welsh Division. Involved 1976–90 in major restructuring of British Steel in Wales, resulting in the reduction of over 40,000 jobs, the closure of obsolete works, and a capital investment programme of some £1.5 billion. Productivity was increased, quality and range of products extended, and costs reduced. Awarded the Sir Robert Hadfield Medal in 1990 by the Institute of Metals. First chairman of West Glamorgan and Dyfed Training and Enterprise Council. Former chairman of the Board of the West Glamorgan Health Authority, chairman of Morriston NHS Trust, and member of the Council of the University of Wales. Member of the Board of British Rail. Trustee of the Trustee Savings Bank Foundation for England and Wales and of the Boys' Clubs of Wales Diamond Jubilee Charitable Trust. President of Côr Meibion Aberafan and of the Port Talbot Amateur Operatic Society, vice-president of Côr Meibion De Cymru and of Aberavon Rugby Football Club.

Recreations: rugby, cricket, music and gardening.

Family motto *Ymdrechu i lwyddo* ('Strive to succeed'). Family roots are in Yorkshire.

DEREK WILLIAM CHARLES MORGAN

BA (Hons.), FIMC, FBIM, DL

Born: 1934, Bargoed.
Educated: Neath Grammar School;
University of Nottingham.
Married: Anne Yvette Davies, two
daughters.

National service in the Royal Engineers 1956–58.

Held management posts in Littlewoods Ltd 1958–61, Ilford Ltd 1961–67. PA Consulting Group 1967–90, main board director responsible for Midlands, West and Wales. In 1990 formed Derek Morgan Partnership and is chairman of Abtrust Preferred Income Investment Trust, PA Pension Scheme, Ogwr and Taff-Ely Partnership Trust, Mid Glamorgan Education Business Partnership, St David's Hall Trust, Bridgend and District NHS Trust and the Prince's Youth Business Trust. Also vice-chairman of the Mid Glamorgan Training and Enterprise Council. Other directorships include Morganite Electrical Carbon Ltd and Moulded Foams (Wales) Ltd. President of the Cardiff Chamber of Commerce and Industry 1990–91. Liveryman of the Welsh Livery Guild.

Recreations: walking the dogs, reading and cricket.

His family background lies in the Rhymney Valley.

HAROLD JOHN TAMPLIN

OBE

Born: 1935, Rudry.
Educated: Caerphilly Grammar School.
Married: Olwyn Mary Owens, one daughter, one son.

A life-long farmer at Cwmnofydd, Rudry, which was farmed by his grandfather in the late nineteenth century, and has now grown from 80 acres to 512 acres. Active with the Young Farmers' Club; awarded a travelling scholarship to Canada in 1960. Member of the National Farmers' Union Council 1974–85. Member of the Secretary of State for Wales's Agricultural and Hill Farming Advisory Panels, and of the Minister of Agriculture's Hill Farming Advisory Panel. Council delegate for the Royal Agricultural Benevolent Institution, and member of the Tredegar Memorial Trust. Much concerned with local affairs.

Recreations: all aspects of the countryside. Plays golf and watches sport, but a busy farmer has limited leisure.

The family was formerly involved in the iron and steel industry. Llanelly Hill churchyard, on the old border between Brecknockshire and Monmouthshire, contains graves of Tamplin forebears.

ISLWYN THOMAS REES

Born: 1930, Pencoed.
Educated: Pencoed Secondary School.
Married: Frances Morgan, twin sons and one daughter.

A farmer from a farming family. Engaged in dairy farming until 1965, then, after purchasing an adjoining farm, moved to Tan-y-Lan and extended into cereal-growing, cattle-rearing and poultry farming. Now in partnership with his son, Paul, in an enterprise consisting of sheep-breeding and fattening, with some beef cattle and arable crops. Founder member and past chairman of the Farmers' Club of Glamorgan; past chairman of branch, and executive member at county level of the National Farmers' Union. Council member of the Royal Welsh Agricultural Society, representative on its board of management and chairman of the Glamorgan Advisory Committee 1986–88.

Recreations: patron of Bridgend Rugby Club, and plays golf.

The family came into Glamorgan in 1840 from Pembrokeshire.

DAVID EDWARD COX

LVO (for services during the visit of HM The Queen to Sri Lanka), MBE, Dato Perduka Makota Brunei (2nd class) awarded by the Sultan of Brunei.

Born: 1932, Wokingham, Berkshire, of Welsh parents.
Educated: Frimley and Camberley Grammar School; Royal Military Academy, Sandhurst.
Married: Nancy Westcott, one son.

After a brief period in the Official Solicitor's Department, Royal Courts of Justice, was called up for national service in 1951 in the Royal Welch Fusiliers. Transferred to the regular army and Sandhurst. Commissioned into The Welch Regiment 1953. Service in Hong Kong, Germany, and in Cyprus during the emergency. Adjutant 1st Battalion The Welch Regiment in Berlin 1961–63, during the Berlin Wall crisis. Commanded the 3rd (Volunteer) Battalion The Royal Regiment of Wales in Cardiff 1974–76. After command and before his retirement in 1983, he was deputy commander of the Ulster Defence Regiment and defence adviser to Sri Lanka.

Subsequently became director of the Prince of Wales' Committee, a charity which encourages voluntary activity to improve the environment in Wales. Since 1992 honorary colonel of the Glamorgan Army Cadet Force. Liveryman of the Welsh Livery Guild.

Recreations: played rugby at representative level in the army and for Crawshay's Welsh XV. Took part in amateur dramatics in the army, playing the Reverend Eli Jenkins while in Northern Ireland. A keen concert-goer and supporter of St David's Hall, Cardiff. Plays bridge and belongs to Royal Porthcawl Golf Club.

His paternal grandfather was surveyor to Margam Urban District Council. His mother's family came from Creigiau and had coal-mining interests in Glamorgan.

KENNETH MERLIN DAVID JOHNS

OBE, Officer's Cross of the German Order of Merit 1986

Born: 1921, Horsham, Sussex.
Educated: Newcastle-upon-Tyne; Cardiff.
Married: Margaret Kipling.

Served in Merchant Navy 1942–47 in Atlantic, Mediterranean and Indian theatres.

Directorships in British, European and American companies in the oil, engineering, aerospace and construction industries. Active in the CBI, the Design Council, president of the Engineering Employers' Association and the Cardiff Chamber of Commerce. Currently a consultant and adviser to industrial firms. Chairman of the Llandaff Cathedral Restoration Appeal to 1991. Honorary consul of the Federal Republic of Germany since 1975. Freeman of the City of London. Liveryman of the Worshipful Company of Tin Plate Workers alias Wire Workers, and of the Welsh Livery Guild. Churchwarden and parish councillor.

Recreations: gardening, country life and antiques.

Family connections are with Carmarthenshire, but he has strong industrial links with Glamorgan. Has lived for twenty-five years at Pencoed House, Capel Llaniltern, a house dating from the fourteenth century, home to the sheriff of Glamorgan of 1687, and associated with the sheriff of 1546.

Mrs BARBARA MAGDALENE LADBROOKE

Born: 1932, Pantruthyn Fach Farm, Pencoed.
Educated: Howell's School, Llandaff; Monmouthshire Institute of Agriculture.
Married: John Price Ladbrooke, two sons (both in police force), one daughter.

Has been a creamery quality control officer at various centres, instructor at Coed-y-Mwstwr Approved School, Coychurch, and was company director of family business, Bridgend Creamery, until 1991. A part-time farmer and owner/breeder of event horses. Active in the Riding for the Disabled Association; founder and organizer of its Bridgend Group, the members of which demonstrated their skills before HRH the Princess Royal at Longacre Farm in 1984; regional chairman of South Wales Region, 1980–86. Member of the organizing committee for the Monmouthshire Horse Trials. Non-executive member of the Mid Glamorgan Family Health Services Authority. Governor of local primary school. Also an HGV driver.

Recreations: hunting, skiing, gardening, music and bell-ringing.

Her Vaughan forebears farmed in Glamorgan.

Colonel GEORGE FREDERICK KENNETH MORGAN

OBE, MC, OStJ, TD, DL (Monmouthshire 1950, Glamorgan 1964)

Born: 1912, Newport, Monmouthshire.
Died: 1988.
Educated: Clifton College, Bristol.
Married: Rosemary Williams, two daughters, one son.

Served in the army 1939–45 with the 2nd Battalion The Monmouthshire Regiment. Mentioned in dispatches and awarded the MC in action in Europe 1944. First commanding officer of the 2nd Monmouthshire TA after the Second World War.

Qualified as a chartered accountant in 1937, winning the William Quilter prize. Resumed practice after the war, and became senior partner successively in Needham & Culley, R. H. March Son & Co., Mann Judd & Co. and Touche Ross & Co., until his retirement in 1983. Formed the first committee in Wales of the Army Benevolent Fund, and was its chairman until 1985. Chairman of the Finance Committee of the Prince of Wales' Committee in Wales. President of the Institute of Directors in Wales.

Recreations: walking, golf, gardening, travel and collecting antiques.

Moved to Cardiff in 1946 from Monmouthshire. His family roots lie in the Forest of Dean.

ANTHONY SELWYN MARTYN

JP, DL

Born: 1928, Penarth.
Educated: Downside School; Trinity College, Cambridge.
Married: Fiona Elizabeth Lewis, one son, two daughters.

Commissioned into the 1st Duke of Cornwall's Light Infantry (now 1st Light Infantry) and spent national service 1948–49 in Cyprus and East Africa.

Farmed in Somerset before joining the family firm of Martyn Martyn & Co. Ltd, shipowners, Cardiff, in 1959. Returned to farming in 1965 and has worked Tinkinswood, St Nicholas, ever since.

Chairman of the Stallion Committee of the National Light Horse Breeding Society from 1984. MFH Glamorgan Foxhounds 1961–91. Member of the Lord Chancellor's Advisory Panel for South Glamorgan and of the South Wales Police Authority. Chairman of the bench from 1990.

Recreations: riding, golf, reading and music.

Son of Selwyn R. Martyn of Dinas Powis (HS 1945).

JOSEPH GERALD GASKELL

TD

Born: 1916, Cardiff.
Educated: Malvern College.
Married: Maureen Elizabeth Jane Thomas (daughter of Sir William James Thomas, Baronet, LL D, JP, HS 1936), two sons.

Served throughout the Second World War in the Royal Artillery, demobilized as captain.

Joined south Wales brewers, William Hancock & Co. Ltd in 1935, chairman from 1959, until business acquired in 1968 by Bass & Co., then chairman of Welsh Brewers Ltd until retirement in 1975. Chairman of the Brewers' Society 1971–72. Member of Cardiff City Council 1961–69.

Recreations: cinematography, from the mid 1930s until the medium was supplanted by video in the 1980s. Won Amateur Ciné World national competition in 1949. Draws and paints in watercolours.

His great-grandfather, William J. G. C. Gaskell, came to south Wales from Devon in 1855 or 1856, and became a Cardiff councillor in 1866. His grandfather, Colonel Joseph Gaskell, CBE, VD, DL, commanded the 2nd Welsh Brigade, Royal Field Artillery(TF); he was chairman of the Glamorgan Territorial Association, JP, general manager from 1887, later chairman, of William Hancock & Co. Ltd and chairman of the Brewers' Society 1916.

His father, Colonel Joseph Gerald Gaskell, CB, TD, DL, served throughout the First World War in the Royal Artillery, was chairman of the Glamorgan Territorial Association, member of Cardiff City Council 1926–32. Chairman of William Hancock & Co. Ltd 1934–59 (HS 1941).

His cousin, Francis Henry Gaskell, was under sheriff for the county of Glamorgan 1952–74, and for the bailiwick of Glamorgan 1974–85.

FRANCIS EDWARD SUTHERLAND HAYES

DL, awarded the Scouts Gilt Cross for Bravery 1945

Born: 1930, Porthcawl.
Educated: Wycliffe College, Stonehouse;
Treforest School of Mines, Pontypridd;
Jesus College, Cambridge.
Married: Suzanne Reardon-Smith, one
son, three daughters.

National service, sub-lieutenant in the Royal Navy 1950–52.

After an engineering apprenticeship, joined the family firm of R. S. Hayes Ltd, iron and steel merchants, Bridgend. After its disposal, purchased Gresswell Valves Ltd, Birmingham, in 1968. Past chairman of the British Valve Manufacturers' Association. Past deputy chairman of the Wales Board of the Trustee Savings Bank Ltd. Member of Lloyd's. Freeman of the City of London, Liveryman of the Worshipful Company of Farriers. Chairman of the Country Landowners Association Game Fair, Wales 1990. Fellow of the Woodard Corporation. Chairman of the governors of the Cathedral School, Llandaff, governor of the Mountain School, Llansannor, and a churchwarden.

Recreations: sailing, shooting and music.

Brother to Forbes Hayes (HS 1972), q.v.

CHRISTOPHER MICHAEL BRAIN

Born: 1939, Dinas Powis.
Educated: Cheltenham College.
Married: Dianne Mary Davies, two daughters, two sons.

Joined S. A. Brain & Co. Ltd as a pupil brewer in 1958. Appointed director in 1968, joint managing director in 1979, chairman in 1989. Over the years the company has expanded its trading area from the Cardiff district to the whole of England and south and west Wales. Chairman of the South Wales Brewers' Association 1987–90, member of the Council of the Brewers' Society. Chairman of Cardiff Crime Prevention Panel 1984–87. Chairman of the governors of Tockington Manor School, 1987 to date. Freeman of the City of London. Liveryman of the Worshipful Company of Brewers, and of the Welsh Livery Guild.

Recreations: cricket, rugby, hockey, shooting and walking.

A great-grandson of J. B. Brain of Kingswood, Bristol, who was one of the co-founders of S. A. Brain & Co. in Cardiff in 1882. Grandson of W. H. Brain of Cwrt-yr-ala, Michaelston-le-Pit, and great-great-nephew of S. A. Brain, the first of the family to settle in south Wales in 1862.

HAROLD EMMOTT WILLIAMS

OBE, BSc

Born: 1925, Edmonton, Alberta, Canada; a
Canadian citizen.
Educated: University of Alberta,
Edmonton, Alberta, and University of
Western Ontario, London, Ontario.
Married: Margaret Marlatt, two daughters.

Commissioned in the Royal Canadian Navy (R).

Joined the family firm of John Williams and Sons (Cardiff) Ltd in 1950 and was its chairman from 1965 until retirement in 1983. Past national president of the Institute of British Foundrymen and of the National Association of Iron and Steel Stockholders and of the Management Research Group of the British Institute of Management. Member of the EEC Iron and Steel Council in Luxembourg. Chairman of the CBI (Wales) 1978–80. Member of the Court of the University of Wales, and of the Council of University College, Cardiff, of which his grandfather had been a founding member. Involved in fund-raising for church and charities, and continues a strong family tradition of association with industrial and educational activities. Liveryman of the Welsh Livery Guild.

Recreations: swimming, golf, reading and enjoying the company of five grandsons.

Grandson of Lewis Williams of Cardiff, JP, and of his redoubtable wife, Mary Ann Elizabeth Jane Morgan of East Barry House, a benefactress to the Wesleyan Methodist cause in the area.

HENRY GETHIN LEWIS

MA (Oxon.), JP, DL

Born: 1933, Penarth.
Educated: Shrewsbury School; Trinity College, Oxford.
Married: Bridget Lovell, one son, one daughter.

National service, sub-lieutenant in the RNVR.

Director of private companies, mostly engineering. Past president of the National Federation of Vehicle Traders. Past member of the Council of the CBI. Past chairman of the Boys' Clubs of Wales.

Recreations: golf, cricket, shooting and fishing.

Grandson of Henry Gethin Lewis (HS 1920), son of Squadron-Leader Henry Gethin Lewis, RAFVR (HS 1958), and brother of Mrs Joanna Cory (HS South Glamorgan 1994).

Sir CHRISTOPHER (MATTHEW) PETERSON

Knight Bachelor, CBE, OStJ, TD, JP, DL

Born: 1918, Cardiff, the ninth of eleven children.
Educated: St Illtyd's College, Cardiff; Cardiff Technical College.
Married: Grace McNeil, two sons (one deceased), one daughter.

Served in the Royal Army Service Corps 1940–46 in West Africa and in India; on demobilization held rank of captain. Active in TA 1946–77, honorary colonel 157 Regiment Royal Corps of Transport.

Joined South Wales India Rubber Co. Ltd as manager in 1946, was appointed director in 1952, developing the company into a broad-based marketing and distribution organization covering the UK. Appointed chairman in 1968 of the SWIRCO-Newton Group until he negotiated its sale to Dorada Holdings PLC in 1979 and joined the board as non-executive director. Chairman of several photographic companies. Member of Cardiff City Council 1968–71 and of South Glamorgan County Council 1973–85.

Appointed president of the Conservative Party in Wales 1991.

Recreations: sport and voluntary organizations.

His father, the son of a Swedish shipbuilder, sailed into Cardiff in the 1890s, married an Irish-born wife and settled in the town.

IVAN DALE OWEN

DL, M.Arch, SP Dip(Hons), FRIBA, FRTPI, FRSA

Born: 1924, Merthyr Tydfil.
Educated: Whitchurch Grammar School; Welsh School of Architecture, Cardiff; School of Planning, London; Massachusetts Institute of Technology; Harvard University, Cambridge, Mass., as Smith-Mundt and Fulbright scholar.
Married: Maureen Kelly, three sons (one deceased).

Served in the Home Guard Heavy Anti-Aircraft Unit 1941–43, and saw action at Cardiff gun sites at Western Avenue and Ely Race Course. Royal Artillery 1943–47 in the UK and India, commanded a gun troop at the North-west Frontier in one of the last British regiments to serve there.

Architect for a wide range of buildings for education, health, industry, commerce and housing, together with urban renewal and planning within many British cities and abroad. Work in Wales includes university master plans for Cardiff, Swansea and Aberystwyth; BBC Headquarters, Llandaff; Welsh Folk Museum, St Fagans; University Pre-Clinical Departments, Cathays Park, Cardiff; Great Hall and Bell Tower, Aberystwyth; factories for Parke-Davis, Pontypool, and Laura Ashley, Newtown; home for the aged in Porthcawl.

Retired as senior Welsh partner, Percy Thomas Partnership, in 1990, and continues in practice, with his wife, as independent consultants. Served as council member of RIBA and president of the Society of Architects in Wales. At present is the chairman of the Civic Trust for Wales and is involved in national and local organizations to conserve and improve the quality of our built environment. Liveryman of the Welsh Livery Guild.

Publications include articles in professional journals, technical and planning reports, various contributions including, most recently, the chapter on architecture in *The New Wales* (University of Wales Press, 1990).

Recreations: music, books, urban landscapes and cycling.

His paternal grandfather moved from north Pembrokeshire to Glamorgan in the late nineteenth century; his maternal forebears were from Newtown, Montgomeryshire.

IAN ERIC COLSTON

JP, DL, MA (Cantab.), FRICS, ACIArb, FAAV, IRRV

Born: 1934, London.
Educated: evacuated to the United States for the duration of the war. North Canton Grade School, Ohio, USA; Ridley College, St Catherine's, Ontario, Canada; Trinity College, Glenalmond, Perth, Scotland; Trinity Hall, Cambridge.
Married: Patricia Ann Turnbull of Llantwit Major, two sons, two daughters.

The sheriff, photographed with his brother, His Honour Judge Colin Colston QC, in the Sheriff's Room, the Law Courts, Cardiff.

National service in the Royal Navy 1952–54, as navigating officer.

Joined W. H. Cooke & Arkwright, Bridgend, then Alfred Savill & Sons, chartered surveyors, Lincoln's Inn Fields, and Valuation Office, Inland Revenue, Cardiff. A chartered surveyor, principal of Colston & Colston. Freeman of the City of London. Liveryman of the Worshipful Company of Chartered Surveyors and of the Welsh Livery Guild. Director and treasurer of the National Welsh American Foundation.

Recreations: shooting and fishing, watching sports, particularly rugby and tennis.

Brought to Glamorgan by his career in 1957. The Colston family can be traced in the Stroud area of Gloucestershire in the seventeenth, eighteenth and nineteenth centuries and to forebears in Westbury-on-Severn in the fifteenth and sixteenth centuries.

CECIL HERBERT RAPPORT

CBE, KStJ, JP, DL

Born: 1915, Cardiff.
Educated: Monkton House College; City of Cardiff Technical College.
Married: Audrey Rachel Fligelstone, one son, two daughters.

Served in The Welch Regiment 1939–46, seconded to a special War Office unit.

Chairman and managing director of M. A. Rapport & Co. Ltd, founded in Cardiff in 1898. Member of Cardiff City Council for seventeen years, alderman, and deputy lord mayor 1970. President of the Cardiff Branch of the Royal British Legion, recipient of the Gold Badge of the National Executive Council of the Royal British Legion. Life patron of the Wales Festival of Remembrance. Founder member of Cardiff Searchlight Tattoo. President of the Friends of Cardiff Royal Infirmary. Past chairman of the Cardiff Appeals Committee of National Children's Homes. President of Cardiff Institute for the Blind. Past president of the Cardiff Chamber of Trade. Ex-trustee and member of the Cardiff New Theatre Trust. An active Scout for many years. Freeman of the City of London, and Liveryman of the Worshipful Company of Horners. Member of the Guild of Freemen of the City of London. Junior warden, the Welsh Livery Guild.

Recreations: boating, swimming and music.

The family has been in Cardiff for five generations.

WILLIAM EMRYS EVANS
CBE, LLD, FCIB, FRSA

Born: 1924, Mallwyd, Merioneth.
Educated: Llanfair Caereinion County School.
Married: Mair Thomas, one daughter.

War service in Royal Navy 1942–46 (mentioned in dispatches).

Career in banking, regional director for Wales of Midland Bank. Director of the Development Board for Rural Wales 1976–89. President of the Royal National Eisteddfod 1980–83. Involved with charitable trusts and foundations. President of the Welsh Congregational Church in Wales 1989. Member of Council and governor of University College, Swansea, and its chairman since 1982; member of the Court and Council of the University of Wales. Trustee of Mansfield College, Oxford, and of Llandovery College. Chairman of the Welsh Sports Aid Foundation.

Recreations: golf, gardening and music.

Moved to Cardiff in 1972 from London, but family roots were in Montgomeryshire.

Sir **BROOKE CHARLES BOOTHBY**, 16th Baronet of Broadlaw Ash

BA (Econ.) (Cantab.)

Born: 1949, Cardiff.
Educated: Eton; Trinity College, Cambridge.
Married: Georgiana Alexandra Russell, two daughters.

Worked for Lysaght Steel Company of New South Wales, Australia, and the Hoburne Leisure Group, UK, before returning to manage the estate surrounding his family home, Fonmon Castle. In addition to mixed farming, the estate carries quarrying and leisure activities such as Fontygary Parks Ltd. Chairman of a number of caravan and tourism-related committees and companies. First chairman of the Historic Houses Association's Inheritance Committee.

Recreations: shooting, gardening and dendrology.

Son of Sir Hugo Boothby (HS 1953), HM Vice-Lieutenant of the county of Glamorgan, HM Lieutenant for the county of South Glamorgan 1974–81. Sir Brooke's ancestor, Colonel Philip Jones (HS 1672), purchased Fonmon Castle in 1656. Members of the Jones family also served the shrievalty in 1683, 1704, 1729, 1801 and 1838.

Sir DONALD WALTERS

Knight Bachelor, LLB

Born: 1925, Swansea.
Educated: Howard Gardens High School for Boys, Cardiff; London School of Economics and Political Science.
Married: Jean McQuistin, one son.

War service as a 'Bevin Boy', underground at Lewis Merthyr colliery, Trehafod, 1944–46.

Called to the Bar by the Inner Temple 1946; practised on the Wales and Chester Circuit 1948–59.

Closely associated with Sir Julian Hodge and development of his national banking and finance house. Deputy managing director, Chartered Trust PLC 1975–85. Member of Cardiff City Council 1955–63. Chairman of Commercial and Industrial Training Services Ltd, a charitable organization providing training for unemployed youths in Mid Glamorgan, South Glamorgan and Gwent. Deputy chairman of the Board of the Welsh Development Agency 1984–93. Member of the executive committee of the Wales Council for Voluntary Action, its chairman 1987–93. President of the Friends of the Rhondda Heritage Park. Chairman of the Council of University of Wales College of Cardiff. Vice-chairman of the Welsh National Opera Board. Vice-chairman of the 1992 National Garden Festival, Ebbw Vale. Chairman of Llandough Hospital NHS Trust.

Recreations: gardening and walking.

The Walters family comes from the Swansea area and is also represented in the neighbourhood of Neath and the Swansea Valley.

DUDLEY HENRY FISHER

CBE, DL, IPFA, CIGasE, CIMgt

Born: 1922, Norwich, Norfolk.
Educated: City of Norwich School.
Married: 1. Barbara Lilian Sexton (died 1984), one son, two daughters.
2. Jean Mary Livingstone Miller.

Served in the Royal Air Force as a pilot 1941–46, flying various aircraft from Tiger Moths to Lancasters, and Ansons to DC3 Dakotas.

In 1948 joined Eastern Electricity Board. In 1953 entered the gas industry, joined Wales Gas Board in 1956, became regional chairman in 1974 and retired in 1987. Chairman of the CBI Welsh Council 1987–89. Chairman of the British National Committee of the World Energy Conference's International Administrative Committee until 1989. Member of the Council of University College, Cardiff, and of the Executive Commission overseeing its merger with the University of Wales Institute of Science and Technology. Member of the Council of University of Wales College of Cardiff. Trustee of Help the Aged charity and chairman of its Overseas Operations Committee. A governor of Atlantic College, St Donat's, and a deputy chairman of the Institute of Welsh Affairs. Vice-chairman of Help Age International; member of the Council of University of Wales College of Medicine. Liveryman of the Welsh Livery Guild.

Recreations: reading, gardening, golf and music.

From a family of Norfolk origin, he was the first of his line to come to south Wales.

CHRISTOPHER LESLIE POLLARD
OBE, FHCIMA

Born: 1939, Twickenham, Middlesex.
Educated: Thames Valley Grammar
School, Twickenham; Ealing School of
Hotel Management; University of Wales
Institute of Science and Technology.
Married: Vivien Mary Hornby, one
daughter.

A lecturer in hotel management at Cardiff College of Food Technology and Commerce before moving into hotel management at the Mount Sorrel Hotel, Barry, and into catering as Hamard Catering Ltd where activity included working with Unilever in the exporting of 8 million school meals to Saudi Arabia. Built and operated two school-meals packaging factories in Saudi Arabia, handling 30 million meals a year. Former chairman of Taste of Wales – Blas ar Gymru Ltd, a marketing organization for Welsh food and food products. Member of Wales Tourist Board, 1983–92. Liveryman of the Worshipful Company of Tin Plate Workers alias Wire Workers, and Freeman of the City of London.

Recreations: travel, hospitality and entertaining; he has recently acquired fluency in Spanish.

His father was a pharmacist by profession; both his paternal and maternal grandfathers were postmen in Great Yarmouth, Norfolk.

BRIAN KEITH THOMAS

Born: 1935, Cardiff.
Educated: Penarth Grammar School.
Married: Ann Jones, one son, one daughter.

National service in Royal Air Force 1953–55.

After work with major insurance companies and pension consultants, he formed B. K. Thomas and Partners Ltd, insurance brokers, in 1970. Chairman of Cardiff Business Club, a director of Cardiff Bay Development Corporation, council member of the Countryside Council for Wales, trustee of the Civic Trust for Wales, member of the board of the Prince's Youth Business Trust, South and West Wales, a member of the Council and of the Court of Governors of the National Museum of Wales, a founding trustee of Cardiff Bay Art Trust. Director and chairman of Middleton Botanic Garden Ltd. Freeman of the City of London, Liveryman of the Worshipful Company of Horners, Liveryman of the Worshipful Company of Tin Plate Workers alias Wire Workers, and Liveryman of the Welsh Livery Guild.

Recreations: collecting antiques, mainly eighteenth-century furniture, silver and porcelain; cricket and rugby football.

Paternal forebears come from Llanybyther, Carmarthenshire, and maternal grandparents from Bristol.

MICHAEL JOHN CLAY

OStJ, FCA

Born: 1929, Cowbridge.
Educated: Winchester College.
Married: 1. Anne Mary Amelia
Gillespie, one daughter, one son.
2. Catherine Vivian Lindsay
Picton-Turbervill, née Corkery.

National service 1947–49, commissioned in The Welch Regiment.

Trained as a chartered accountant in south Wales, specializing in smaller businesses. A former president of the South Wales Society of Chartered Accountants. Chairman of Llandaff Diocesan Board of Finance, churchwarden and treasurer of Llansannor parish church. Agent for the Conservative candidate, Pontypridd division, in 1974 election, and stood as candidate in 1979. Treasurer of the Priory for Wales of the Most Venerable Order of the Hospital of St John of Jerusalem.

Recreations: training gun dogs, shooting, forestry and amateur operatics.

Eldest son of J. C. Clay, who played cricket for Glamorgan 1921–50, and for England against South Africa in 1936. The family originated in Staffordshire and Derbyshire, but was more recently in Chepstow, Monmouthshire. His grandfather, Charles Leigh Clay, had a coal-exporting business out of Cardiff Docks in the 1890s. He was HS Monmouthshire in 1926. An uncle, Henry Patrick Clay, was HS Monmouthshire in 1965, and another uncle, Gerald Leigh Clay, HS Herefordshire in 1950.

ALASTAIR OWEN GOLLEY

Born: 1933, Romford, Essex.
Educated: King's College School, Wimbledon.
Married: Margaret Helen King, one son, one daughter.

National service with the Royal Electrical and Mechanical Engineers.

After an early career in the City and in Marks and Spencer, became founder and chief executive of Golley Slater Group Ltd, a multi-disciplined marketing services group, in advertising, marketing and public relations. Founder signatory of the Community Investment Charter, former member of the Sports Council for Wales, member of the Development Committee of the MacIntyre Foundation (which offers a full life to the mentally disabled), active in fund-raising for various charities.

Recreations: tennis, squash, opera and wine.

Came to Cardiff in 1958. The family originates from the area of the Roseland peninsula in Cornwall.

JOHN MASCALL DARBY CURTEIS

RD*, FCA, DL

Born: 1941, Inverness, Scotland.
Educated: Radley College.
Married: Fiona Pexton, two daughters,
one son.

Trained and qualified as a chartered accountant with Whinney Smith & Whinney/Whinney Murray & Co., London. Transferred to Cardiff office on its formation, becoming partner from 1974 in Ernst & Whinney/Ernst & Young. Took early retirement to work as an independent business consultant. Chairman of South and East Wales Ambulance NHS Trust. Commander in Royal Naval Reserve, commanding officer HMS *Cambria* 1988–92. President of Barry Branch of the Royal Naval Association and of the Porthcawl Sea Cadet Unit. Vice-chairman (Navy) of TAVRA for Wales. Treasurer of the Wales Chamber of Commerce and Industry, the Cardiff Branch of NSPCC, the Bosses' Walk Committee of Welsh Sports Aid, and the South Glamorgan Community Foundation. Past president of Cardiff Chamber of Commerce and Industry and of the South Wales Chartered Accountants Students' Society. Past chairman of the Cardiff Committee of King George's Fund for Sailors and of St Fagan's Village Association. Member of the Council of the Order of St John, South Glamorgan, and of the Gwerin Housing Association Management Committee. Freeman of the City of London, Liveryman of the Worshipful Company of Feltmakers and of the Welsh Livery Guild.

Recreations: theatre, music, gardening, fishing and sailing.

Has Glamorgan forebears through Paulina, daughter of Sir John Godfrey Thomas, 6th Baronet, formerly of Wenvoe Castle, who married, in 1848, Herbert Mascall Curteis of Windmill Hill and Peasmarsh Place, Sussex.

ALAN BURNYEAT TURNBULL

OBE, BSc, FRAgS

Born: 1907, Loweswater, Cumberland.
Died: 1990.
Educated: Doncaster Grammar School; Leeds University.
Married: Myfanwy Evans, one daughter.

Lecturer in agriculture at Leeds University 1932–34, and for Ministry of Agriculture 1934–45. Took up farming in 1945, working more than 1,000 acres on Penrice Home Farm and at Oxwich Castle. Served on the Potato Marketing Board, the National Milk Records Committee, the British Wool Marketing Board and in the National Institute of Agricultural Engineering. Member of the South Wales Shorthorn Breeders' Club and of the Clun Forest Sheep Breeders' Association. He was associated with the Royal Welsh Agricultural Society from 1948, honorary show director from 1967, president in 1969, programme director from 1970 and recipient of its Gold Medal in 1975.

Recreations: shooting and sports.

His family roots are in the north of England.

CLAUD GERALD BELLINGHAM

MA, DL

Born: 1908, Swansea.
Died: 1985.
Educated: Bromsgrove School; Sidney Sussex College, Cambridge.
Married: Margaret Bevan (daughter of Colonel John Maybery Bevan, HS 1929
Carmarthenshire), one son, two daughters.

During the Second World War, served in Small Boats in 1939, and as
communications officer with the Home Guard while in reserved occupations.
Became managing director of John Player & Sons Ltd, tinplate manufacturers,
Clydach, Swansea. Then director of Llanelly Steel during nationalization.
Prominent in scouting, becoming commissioner for South Wales, and involved in
Boys' Club and Sea Scouts' activities in Swansea. Chairman of the General
Purposes Committee of the Representative Body of the Church in Wales and
member of the Electoral College. Chairman of Swansea and District Branch of the
RSPCA.

Recreations: sailing (rear-commodore of Bristol Channel Yacht Club), veteran car
restoration and the Brighton Run, bird-watching, farming, dogs and photography.

His great-grandfather came to Wales from Sussex to practise law in partnership
with J. Strick. His maternal great-grandfather was medical officer in Swansea in
the nineteenth century.

MARTIN THOMAS

OBE, CStJ, JP, DL

Born: 1924, Skewen, Neath.
Educated: Dumbarton House School, Swansea.
Married: Dorothy Louise Callway (died 1992), one daughter.

Served in the Royal Air Force 1944–45, and in the Royal Army Medical Corps 1945–47.

Returned to his family business in 1947. Chairman and managing director of David Thomas, Sons & Co. Ltd, builders' merchants, and of Gwern Estates Ltd. Served extensively in local government, on Neath Rural District Council 1961–73, Neath Borough Council 1973–79, Glamorgan County Council 1964–74, and West Glamorgan County Council from 1973, becoming the senior serving county member. Mayor of Neath Borough, 1977–78.

A member of the South Wales Police Authority from 1973. Appointed JP in 1965, chairman of the Neath bench 1984–87. Member of the Magistrates' Courts' Committee for Glamorgan 1969–73, and of the West Glamorgan Magistrates' Courts' Committee from 1973, its chairman 1982–94. Glamorgan, and later West Glamorgan, representative on the central council of magistrates' courts' committees from 1969, the most senior council member in the United Kingdom.

President of the West Wales Rugby Union, of the Central Glamorgan Rugby Union, and of the Neath and Skewen Clubs.

Recreations: reading, politics, rugby football and travel.

Both his paternal and maternal forebears were of farming stock from Brechfa, Carmarthenshire.

ROBERT CAMERON HASTIE

CBE, RD, JP, DL 1974–91, HM Vice Lord-Lieutenant for the county of West Glamorgan from 1991

Born: 1933, Swansea.
Educated: Bromsgrove School.
Married: Mary Griffiths, two sons, one daughter.

National service in the Royal Navy 1951–53. Joined the Royal Naval Reserve and rose through progressive ranks to captain RNR in command of HMS *Cambria*, the South Wales Reserve Division 1974–77. ADC to HM The Queen 1977, and commodore RNR 1979.

Chairman of family engineering company, Bernard Hastie & Company Ltd, UK and Australia. Chairman of the West Wales Training and Enterprise Council Limited. Active in maritime organizations, including membership of the committee of management of RNLI and of the Search and Rescue Committee RNLI. Chairman of Milford Haven Port Authority, of Mumbles Lifeboat Station Branch Committee and of West Glamorgan Scout Council. President of the Swansea Unit of the Sea Cadet Corps.

Recreations: farming, sailing and shooting.

His great-great-great-grandfather, James Hastie, was born in Dumfriesshire, Scotland, in 1768.

DONALD HUMPHREY DAVIES

JP, DL

Born: 1909, Neath.
Educated: Newbridge Secondary School; Gwent College, Newport.
Married: Vera Waddington, two sons (one deceased).

Joined Richard Thomas & Co., tinplate manufacturers, in 1926. Became, in 1952, general manager of the west Wales section of Richard Thomas & Baldwins Ltd, concerned with steel-making, sheet and tinplate, foundries, engineering and pressworks. After nationalization, the firm's west Wales section became Associated Products and Coatings Division. Responsible for successfully introducing a new product – steel strip coated with plastic paints, called Colorcoat. Retired from the British Steel Corporation in 1973. Past chairman of the Siemens Steel Association and president of the European Coil Coaters' Association based in Brussels. Chairman of the Welsh Association of Youth Clubs, president of Morriston Hospital League of Friends, governor and council member of University College of Swansea.

Recreations: active in rugby, riding, skiing and sailing.

The family has been prominent in the south Wales tinplate industry for three generations; his grandfather Robert Davies was involved in setting up Richard Thomas & Co. in the 1870s, and in managing the Melingriffith Tinplate Co. in Whitchurch.

KEITH CYRIL AUSTIN BAILEY

Born: 1919, Swansea.
Died: 1990.
Educated: Wycliffe College,
Stonehouse.
Married: Joan Thomas, one son.

War service with the Territorial Army in 1939 in 53rd Division of the Royal Army Service Corps, later in 23rd Division. Went to France with British Expeditionary Force. Served in the Far East, captured by Japanese at Singapore in 1942, forced to work on the construction of the Singapore–Bangkok railway.

Main career in family business, Bailey Carpets Ltd, founded in 1887 by his grandfather. Retired in 1987. Member of various business organizations and clubs, active in charitable organizations, including the British Limbless Ex-Servicemen's Association for Swansea and West Wales, the South-west Wales Far East Prisoner-of-War Association. Vice-president of the Wales Council for the Disabled. Involved in church affairs, member of the Governing Body and of the Representative Body of the Church in Wales. Member of the Court of the University of Wales and of the Council of University College, Swansea.

Recreations: motoring, countryside and walking.

While his paternal grandfather founded the family firm in Swansea, his maternal grandfather, Howell Watkins, founded a printing firm in Swansea and served as mayor in 1896.

Sir **MICHAEL ROWLAND GODFREY LLEWELLYN**, Baronet

KStJ, JP, DL 1982–86, HM Vice Lord-Lieutenant for the county of West Glamorgan 1986–87, appointed HM Lord-Lieutenant for the county of West Glamorgan in 1987

Born: 1921, Neath.
Educated: Harrow; Royal Military College, Sandhurst.
Married: 1. Bronwen Mary Williams-Wynn.
2. Janet Prudence Edmondes, three daughters.

Commissioned in the Grenadier Guards 1941. Served in Italian campaign 1943–44, wounded in action. Retired from army 1949. Commanded the 1st Glamorgan Battalion Army Cadet Force 1951–59. Engaged in military organizations, public service and charitable activities. President of TAVRA Wales from 1990. President of West Glamorgan Branches of the British Legion, the Soldiers', Sailors' and Airmens' Families Association, patron of the Normandy Veterans' Association and of the Combined Services Association. President of the Army Cadet Force Association for Wales, of West Glamorgan Magistrates' Association, of West Glamorgan Scout Council and of West Glamorgan Trust for Sick Children. President of the St John Council for West Glamorgan. Active in the Conservative Party in Wales, former president of Gower Conservative Association, president of Mid and West Wales Conservative European Association. Liveryman of the Welsh Livery Guild.

Recreations: shooting, gardening and motor racing (in earlier days).

Son of Sir Robert Godfrey Llewellyn (HS Glamorgan 1947, Monmouthshire 1963), who was created a baronet in 1959. The Llewellyn family of Baglan and Court Colman also provided sheriffs for the county in 1852, 1854 and 1925, and traces its ancestry to farming stock in Pentre, Ystradyfodwg, in the early eighteenth century.

ALEXANDER HERBERT LINDSEY ECCLES

Born: 1908, Neath.
Died: 1991.
Educated: Repton.
Married: Doris Anne Kitt, two step-daughters.

Served in the Suffolk Yeomanry, in the Middle East and France. Twice mentioned in dispatches.

A Grand Prix racing driver at Brooklands, Donnington and the Isle of Man, driving Bugattis. In 1934 awarded the Inston Trophy after winning the greatest number of races during the season. After retiring from racing became managing director of Briton Ferry Steelworks, but took up farming in the 1950s. Chairman of the Gower Commoners for twenty-five years, a master bee-keeper and member of the Bristol Channel Yacht Club. Patron of Swansea Motor Club and a life member of the British Racing Drivers' Club. Involved with raising funds for provisions for the disabled.

Recreations: his fine collection of birds' eggs, containing examples of all but twelve species in the UK, is now in Swansea Museum.

Brought up in Carmarthenshire, the son of Herbert Eccles of Neath (HS 1905), who founded the Briton Ferry Steelworks in the late 1880s, and whose collection of porcelain is in the Glynn Vivian Art Gallery, Swansea.

ARTHUR GORDON CHILCOTT

FCA

Born: 1925, Swansea.
Died: 1990.
Educated: Monkton Coombe School, Bath; Swansea Grammar School.
Married: Margaret Olive Thomas, JP.

After qualifying as an accountant, joined family firm of hardware and oil distributors in south and west Wales. Founder member, chairman and president of Abbeyfield (Swansea) Society Ltd. Vice-president of the Glynn Vivian Home of Rest for the Blind. A Swansea county borough/city councillor, and West Glamorgan county councillor.

Recreations: fly-fishing, shooting, photography, astronomy, travel and reading.

His father, Arthur Chilcott, a well-known lay preacher, came to Swansea from Devon. His mother's family was from Gower.

DAVID HUNTER ANDREWS

BA, FICA

Born: 1930, Cardiff.
Educated: Radley College;
University College, Cardiff.
Married: Diana Watts, one son, two
daughters.

Served in the Royal Artillery in Hong Kong.

Worked in family company, David Evans & Co. (Swansea) Ltd, 1956–78; now practises as a chartered accountant. Director of development, leisure and investment companies. A past president of the South Wales and Monmouthshire Society of Chartered Accountants.

Recreations: golf, tennis, bridge and art-collecting. A past president of the Welsh Squash Racquets Association.

A descendant of Solomon Andrews, who moved to Cardiff from Wiltshire in the 1840s and set up in business, assisted by his sons. Solomon Andrews became an entrepreneur in many business fields, shops, cars, as a funeral director, and as a builder in developing Cardiff and its neighbourhood, as well as at Pwllheli, north Wales. The family was noted as collectors of art, porcelain and ivories.

BRIAN BRENDAN HICKEY

TD, JP, MA, MCh (Oxon.), FRCS(Eng.)

Born: 1912, Hyde, Cheshire. *Educated*: Manchester Grammar School; University College, Oxford; the London Hospital.
Married: Marjorie Flynn, one son, two daughters.

Commissioned in the Royal Army Medical Corps (TA) in 1939, serving as a surgical specialist, first in the UK and 1942–45 in India. Demobilized in 1945, a lieutenant-colonel. Continued in Territorial service. Commanding officer, colonel, to 3rd Western General Hospital TA 1962–67. Honorary colonel to 203 General Hospital TAVR 1974–78. President of the South Wales Branch of the British Limbless Ex-Servicemen's Association.

Consultant surgeon to Iraq government 1946–48, and surgeon from 1948 at Morriston, Gorseinon and Singleton hospitals. Professor of surgery at the University of Khartoum 1952–55. Honorary surgeon to HM The Queen 1965–67. Hunterian Professor, the Royal College of Surgeons of England 1958.

Recreations: travel, hill and mountain walking.

Roots outside Wales, the first of his line in Swansea.

EDWARD GWYNNE THOMAS
JP, DL

Born: 1921, Gowerton.
Died: 1990.
Educated: Jones' West Monmouthshire
School, Pontypool
Married: Joan Barrett.

Served in the Royal Air Force, 1940–46.

Joined Lloyds Bank in 1938 and held positions in Swansea, Salisbury, Leicester and Aylesbury. Retired in 1981 as regional general manager. Director of the South Wales Board of Lloyds Bank 1981–86. A past president of the Institute of Bankers. Founder chairman of West Glamorgan Enterprise Trust 1982–88. A JP in Swansea in 1969 and subsequently in Leicester, Buckinghamshire and West Glamorgan. Member of the Court and Council of University College, Swansea. Treasurer to many local societies.

Recreations: reading, cricket, rugby football and golf.

His family roots lie in the area of west Glamorgan.

EDEN MARTIN HUGHES EVANS

JP, DL

Born: 1938, Gorseinon.
Educated: Llanelli Grammar School; St Michael's School, Bryn, Llanelli (a school founded by a nephew of Benjamin Hughes and where his mother was the first pupil).
Married: Siani Jenkins, two daughters.

Entered family business, Ben Hughes Loughor foundry, which had been established in 1864 by his great-grandfather, Benjamin Hughes, to supply local collieries and tinworks. In the 1930s engineering was introduced and further expansion took place after the war. Although the foundry section has now been closed, as the demand for castings by smaller steelworks has decreased, engineering activities have been expanded and continue today.

Recreations: rugby football and railways, especially the Great Western Railway. President of Loughor Rugby Football Club. Trustee of Llanelli Rugby Football Club.

His maternal Hughes forebear, according to family tradition, came to Loughor from Dowlais, bringing expertise in ironfounding. His paternal Evans line was from Ammanford, Carmarthenshire. His father was divisional education officer in Llanelli and further education officer for Carmarthenshire.

PHILIP RICHARD VERNON WATKINS

JP, FRICS

Born: 1930, Sketty, Swansea.
Educated: Leighton Park School,
Reading.
Married: Lilian Effie Barron, three
daughters, one son.

National service commissioned in the Royal Artillery 1953–55.

A chartered surveyor, a partner in the family business founded by his father, Jno. Oliver Watkins, in 1920. Retired in 1988. National president of the Royal Institution of Chartered Surveyors 1981–82, chairman of Swansea Building Society 1992 and vice-commodore of the Bristol Channel Yacht Club 1990. Chairman of the National Society for the Protection of Children from Cruelty's child protection team support group.

Recreations: gardening and non-serious golf.

The family has been associated with Swansea since the turn of the century, but originated from Myddfai, Carmarthenshire.

Dr STUART POOLE JENKINS
LRCP, LRCS, LRCPS, DObstRCOG

Born: 1936, Gorseinon.
Educated: St Michael's School, Bryn, Llanelli; Ellesmere College, Shropshire; Medical School, University of Manchester; Royal College of Surgeons in Ireland.
Married: Gillian Mary Bowen, two daughters, one son.

A doctor in general practice in Gorseinon; clinical assistant, Gorseinon Hospital; medical adviser, Lliw Valley Borough Council; chairman of West Glamorgan Local Medical Committee; medical officer, Department of Health and Social Security. Member of the Governing Body of the Church in Wales.

Recreations: rugby, cricket, golf, walking, reading and travel.

The family has been resident in the county since 1920, and came from the Lampeter area of Cardiganshire.

BRIAN KAY DAVISON

OBE, BSc, PhD, CChem, FRSC, CEng, FIMM

Born: 1926, Newcastle-upon-Tyne.
Educated: Dame Allan's School
(Cathedral School), Newcastle-
upon-Tyne; King's College,
University of Durham.
Married: Pamela Jean Williams,
two sons.

Worked as a technical officer in the Agricultural Division of ICI and for the British West Indies Sugar Research Scheme in Trinidad. Joined Inco Europe Ltd in 1962, and in 1965 transferred to their Clydach refinery. Became general manager in 1975, director and general manager in 1978 and production director of Inco Europe Ltd in 1982. Retired 1991. President of the Gower Division of the Scout Association, a governor of the University of Wales, and a former governor and council member of the University College of Swansea. Member of the executive committee of the Swansea Festival of Music and the Arts.

Recreations: squash, tennis, skiing and golf. In younger days played rugby for, and captained, Northumberland county.

Family roots lie in Northumberland.

JOHN BRIAN DICKINSON SIMPSON

JP, FCIB

Born: 1926, Swansea.
Educated: Swansea Grammar School.
Married: Margaret Hilary Saunders, one son, one daughter.

Served in Royal Artillery 1944–47, mostly in India.

Pursued a career in banking in Swansea and the west of England between 1948 and his retirement in 1986. Treasurer to numerous philanthropic, public service and learned bodies, including the Royal Institution of South Wales, and also Swansea Cricket and Football Club. Member of the Court of the University of Wales, and of the Council of the University College of Swansea.

Recreations: played cricket, rugby and tennis, and refereed rugby until the age of forty. Now plays golf, not too seriously. Collects antiques, books, memorabilia; is a modest pianist and supports opera, musical comedy and the Swansea Festival of Music and the Arts, of which he is the current honorary secretary.

The family moved to Swansea in the mid-nineteenth century from Plymouth, but was originally from Scotland.

Dr EDWARD MORGAN ROBERTS

MBBCh, MRCGP

Born: 1945, north Gower.
Educated: Gowerton Boys'
Grammar School; Welsh National
School of Medicine, Cardiff.
Married: Anne Williams, two sons.

After hospital posts in Cardiff Royal Infirmary and East Glamorgan Hospital, entered general practice in Port Talbot in 1972. Member and past chairman and past secretary of West Glamorgan Local Medical Committee. Past member and past chairman of Dyffryn Comprehensive School governing body. Vice-chairman of the West Glamorgan Division of the British Medical Association. Medical officer for Aberavon Rugby Football Club.

Recreations: gardening, reading and mountain-biking.

Forebears in north Gower include carpenters and coal-miners.

WILLIAM ISAAC JAMES

MBE

Born: 1936, Treboeth, Swansea.
Educated: Swansea Technical
School.
Married: Margaret Davies, three
sons.

An engineering apprenticeship with ICI (Metals Division) at Landore Copper Works was followed by training at the newly constructed (1957) titanium factory at Waunarlwydd and two years at sea as an engineering officer with the Union Castle Line.

In 1961, he returned to the Waunarlwydd factory, which was in the forefront in developing processes and applications to exploit the benefits of titanium. Appointed works director in 1979. The factory employed 500 people on an 80-acre site, and supplied the aerospace, nuclear, chemical and power-generation industries, meeting rigorous quality and inspection standards. Retired in 1991.

Served on the Court of Governors of University College, Swansea, and on the West Wales Committee of the CBI.

Recreations: rugby, DIY, sailing and amateur operatics.

Both paternal and maternal sides of the family have roots in west Glamorgan, the paternal line having moved into the industrial area from Carmarthenshire at the end of the nineteenth century.

ALAN CHARLES AYLESBURY

OBE, CEng, MIMechE

Born: 1936, Monmouthshire.
Educated: Grammar Technical
School, Abertillery; Technical
College of Monmouthshire;
University of Wales Institute of
Science and Technology.
Married: 1. by first marriage one
son, one daughter.
2. Maureen Summerfield, née Price,
one stepson, one stepdaughter.

Held engineering posts in steel industry engaged on multi-million-pound rolling mill developments in Wales and elsewhere in the UK. Works engineer of High Duty Alloys Rolling Mill Division and chief mechanical engineer at Ebbw Vale Steelworks. In 1976 joined Alcoa as engineering manager responsible for the final installation and commissioning of £40 million investment on advanced technology rolling mills. Subsequently production manager and rolled products business manager. Managing director from 1981.

President of the Aluminium Federation of Great Britain, 1987–88, director of the Aluminium Federation of Great Britain. Member of the CBI West Wales Council and of the CBI Wales Council. Member of the Wales Innovation and Technology Committee, past member of the Welsh Advisory Board Steering Committee. Past governor and council member of University College of Swansea. Chairman of the West Glamorgan area of the Sir Geraint Evans Heart Research Institute.

Recreations: tennis, swimming, walking and reading.

He is a native of Monmouthshire, whose working career brought him to Glamorgan in 1960. His paternal grandfather came to south Wales from Wiltshire, his maternal grandfather from Somerset, both from rural communities.

Lists of the Sheriffs of
The Lordship of Glamorgan to 1541
The County of Glamorgan 1541–1973
The County of Mid Glamorgan 1974–1994
The County of South Glamorgan 1974–1994
The County of West Glamorgan 1974–1994

Sheriffs of the Lordship of Glamorgan
to 1541

Based on the list published in Volume III of the *Glamorgan County History.*

(R) indicates an appointment made by the Crown when the lordship of Glamorgan and Morgan was in the king's hands.

*c.*1102	William, sheriff of Cardiff
*c.*1126	Ralph, sheriff of Cardiff
*c.*1122–1149	Sir Robert Norreis, Knight
*c.*1149–1183	Robert FitzGregory
*c.*1151	Eiglinus de Purbica
*c.*1170	William de Bosco
*c.*1183	William de Clifford
*c.*1185	Hamo de Valognes
*c.*1200	Henry de Penbridge
*c.*1214	Baldwin de Swineshead
*c.*1214–1216	Ralph de Swineshead
1217	David de Burhill
*c.*1217	Martin
*c.*1217–1230	William de Acra
1233	Ranulph de Hurle (R)
Before 1243	Peter Pincerna
*c.*1243–1245	Stephen Bauzan
1245	William de Wauton
1246	Stephen Bauzan
1249	Geoffrey de Fanencourt
*c.*1250–1260	William de St Elena
1262	Walter de Sully
1266	Bartholomew de la More
*c.*1270–1280	Robert le Veel
1289	John de Crepping

1292	John de Crepping
1293	John de Crepping
*c.*1298	Sir Henry de Penbridge
1299	Simon de Raleye
1300	Simon de Raleye
1302	Simon de Raleye
1304	Simon de Raleye
1305, July	Richard de la Rokele
1307	Robert de Grendon (R)
1313–1314	Robert de Grendon
1314, July	Ingelram Berenger (R)
1314, September	Bartholomew de Badlesmere (R)
1315, July	Robert de Grendon (R)
1315, December	Payn de Turberville (R)
1316, August	Robert de Grendon (R)
1317, May	Robert de Grendon (R)
1319	Sir John Inge
1320–1321	Sir John Inge
1322	Sir John de Inge
1324	Adam de Bowes
1325–1326	Adam de Bowes
1326	Roger de Chandos (R)
1327, March–May	John de Acton (R)
1329	Sir Nicholas de Clare
1330, March	Roger de Chandos (R)
1331	Howel ap Howel
1333	John de Mounteney
1338	Sir William de Erkelowe
1339	Peter Corbet
1344	Sir Mathew le Sore, Knight
1346	Sir Mathew le Sore, Knight
1351	Sir Mathew le Sore, Knight
1358	Sir Gilbert de Ellesfield, Knight
1366	Sir Edward Stradling, Knight
1369	Sir Edward Stradling, Knight
1375	Ralph Seymour (R)
1377	Sir Walter Bluet, Knight (R)
1386, October	Sir William Stradling, Knight
1397	Sir John St John, Knight
1400	Sir John Greyndor, Knight (R)
1414	Sir William Palton, Knight
1421–1423	Sir John Stradling, Knight
1424	Sir Oliver de St John, Knight
1440	Sir William Thomas, Knight
1445	Sir John Beauchamp, Knight
1448	Sir Walter Skull, Knight

1451	Thomas Nevill
1453	Sir William Herbert, Knight
1455	Sir William Herbert, Knight
1460, February	Sir William Herbert, Knight (R)
1477–1485	Sir James Tyrell, Knight
1485, September	Sir Roger Cotton, Knight (R)
1488	Sir Richard Croft, Knight
1509	Charles Somerset, Lord Herbert (created Earl of Worcester in 1514) was appointed sheriff, during the King's pleasure, on 18 May 1509, and for life in August 1509
1526	Henry Somerset (died 1549), Earl of Worcester, succeeded his father as sheriff of Glamorgan, for life, on 15 April 1526. He had been granted the reversion of this office on 25 June 1518

Sheriffs of the County of Glamorgan 1541–1973

Based on the list published by George Williams in *The Sheriffs of Glamorgan*, 1966. The Glamorgan Record Office holds a series of documents relating to shrieval appointments from 1834 onwards.

1541	George Herbert, Esquire [of Swansea]
1542	Sir Rice Mansel, Knight [of Margam]
1543	Sir Edward Carne, Knight [of Ewenny]
1544	William Bassett, Esquire [of Beaupré, St Hilary]
1545	George Mathew [of Radyr Court]
1546	John [Thomas] Bassett [of Llantrithyd]
1547	Miles Mathew [of Llandaff]
1548	Sir Thomas Stradling, Knight [of St Donat's Castle]
1549	Edward Lewis, Esquire [of Van, Caerphilly]
1550	Christopher Turbervill, Esquire [of Penllyn Castle]
1551	James Thomas, Esquire [of Llanmihangel]
1552	William Herbert, Esquire [of Cogan Pill]
1553	Sir George Herbert, Knight [of Swansea]
1554	Sir Rice Mansel, Knight [of Margam]
1555	Sir Edward Carne, Knight [of Ewenny]
1556	Edward Lewis, Esquire [of Van, Caerphilly]
1557	James Button [of Worlton, Duffryn, St Nicholas]
1558	William Bassett, Esquire [of Beaupré, St Hilary]
1559	Sir Richard Walwyn, Knight [of Llantrithyd]
1560	Edward Lewis [of Van, Caerphilly]
1561	John Carne, Esquire [of Nash Manor]
1562	Thomas Carne [of Ewenny]
1563	David Evans [of Great House, Neath]
1564	William Herbert, Esquire, of Swansea
1565	Miles Button, Esquire [of Worlton, Duffryn, St Nicholas]
1566	William Jenkins, Esquire [of Tythegston and Blaen Baglan]
1567	William Herbert, Esquire, of Cogan Pill

1568   William Mathew, Esquire [of Radyr Court]
1569   Christopher Turbervill, Esquire [of Penllyn Castle]
1570   Thomas Lewis, Esquire [of Van, Caerphilly]
1571   Miles Button, Esquire [of Worlton, Duffryn, St Nicholas]
1572   Thomas Carne, Esquire [of Ewenny]
1573   Richard Gwyn [of Llansannor]
1574   Sir Edward Stradling, Knight [of St Donat's Castle]
1575   Edward Kemeys, Esquire [of Cefn Mably]
1576   Sir Edward Mansel, Knight [of Margam]
1577   Nicholas Herbert, Esquire [of Cardiff]
1578   Sir William Herbert, Knight [of Swansea]
1579   John Thomas, Esquire [of Llanmihangel]
1580   William Mathew, Esquire [of Radyr Court]
1581   Thomas Carne, Esquire [of Ewenny]
1582   Sir William Herbert, Knight, of Swansea
1583   Edward Stradling, Esquire [of St Donat's Castle]
1584   George Herbert, Esquire [of Nash]
1585   Edward Kemeys, Esquire [of Cefn Mably]
1586   Nicholas Herbert, Esquire [of Cardiff]
1587   Thomas Lewis, Esquire [of Van, Caerphilly]
1588   John Carne, Esquire [of Ewenny]
1589   Miles Button, Esquire [of Worlton, Duffryn, St Nicholas]
1590   Henry Mathew, Esquire [of Radyr Court]
1591   Anthony Mansel, Esquire [of Llantrithyd]
1592   Sir William Herbert, Knight [of Swansea]
1593   Edmund Mathew, Esquire [of Radyr Court]
1594   Sir Thomas Mansel, Knight [of Margam]
1595   Edward Kemeys, Esquire [of Cefn Mably]
1596   Sir Edward Stradling, Knight [of St Donat's Castle]
1597   Richard Bassett, Esquire [of Beaupré, St Hilary]
1598   John Gwyn, Esquire [of Llansannor] *(died in office)*
1598   Rowland Morgan, Esquire [of Llandaff]
1599   Thomas Lewis, Esquire [of Ruperra]
1600   Edward Prichard, Esquire [of Llancaiach]
1601   John Carne, Esquire [of Ewenny]
1602   Edward Lewis, Esquire [of Van, Caerphilly]
1603   Thomas Aubrey, Esquire [of Llantrithyd]
1604   Sir Thomas Mansel, Knight [of Margam]
1605   Edward Kemeys, Esquire [of Cefn Mably]
1606   William Herbert, Esquire, of Swansea
1607   Sir Rowland Morgan, Knight [of Llandaff]
1608   John Stradling, Esquire [of St Donat's Castle]
1609   Richard Bassett, Esquire [of Beaupré, St Hilary]
1610   Morgan Meirick, Esquire [of Cottrell, St Nicholas]
1611   George Lewis, Esquire [of Llystalybont]
1612   Lewis Thomas, Esquire, of Bettws

1613	Sir Edward Lewis, Knight [of Van, Caerphilly]
1614	Thomas Mathew, Esquire, of Castell-y-Mynach, [Pentyrch]
1615	Gabriel Lewis, Esquire [of Llanishen]
1616	Christopher Turbervill, Esquire [of Penllyn Castle]
1617	David Kemeys, Esquire [of Cefn Mably]
1618	William Mathew, Esquire, of Aberaman, [Aberdare]
1619	Edward Van, Esquire [of Marcross]
1620	Sir John Stradling, Knight and Baronet [of St Donat's Castle]
1621	John Carne, Esquire [of Ewenny]
1622	William Bassett, Esquire [of Beaupré, St Hilary]
1623	Sir Thomas Mansel, Knight and Baronet [of Margam]
1624	Lewis Thomas, Esquire [of Bettws]
1625	Anthony Gwyn [of Llansannor]
1626	William Bawdrip, Esquire [of Splott, Roath]
1627	Edmund Thomas [of Wenvoe Castle]
1628	Henry Mansel, Esquire [of Llanddewi, Gower]
1629	Sir Thomas Lewis, Knight [of Penmark Place]
1630	Thomas Lewis, Esquire [of Llanishen]
1631	Sir Anthony Mansel, Knight [of Briton Ferry]
1632	David Evans, Esquire [of Gnoll, Neath]
1633	Edward Thomas, Esquire [of Llanmihangel]
1634	John Aubrey, Esquire [of Llantrithyd]
1635	Watkin Lougher, Esquire [of Tythegston]
1636	Walter Thomas, Esquire [of Swansea]
1637	Sir Lewis Mansel, Knight and Baronet [of Margam]
1638	Edward Prichard, Esquire, of Llancaiach
1639	Nicholas Kemeys, Esquire, of Cefn Mably
1640	John Carne, Esquire, of Ewenny
1641	Robert Button, Esquire [of Worlton, Duffryn, St Nicholas]
1642	William Bassett of Broviskin [Miskin]
1643	Richard Bassett, Esquire [of Fishweir, St Mary Church, and Aberaman, Aberdare]
1644	Sir Charles Kemeys, Knight and Baronet [of Cefn Mably]
1645	William Thomas [of Dan-y-Graig, Swansea]
1646	Edward Carne, Esquire, of Ewenny
1646	Bussy Mansel, Esquire, of Briton Ferry
1647	Bussy Mansel, Esquire, of Briton Ferry *(continued in office)*
1648	Richard Jones, Esquire [of Michaelston-super-Ely]
1649	John Price, Esquire [of Gellihir, Ilston]
1650	John Herbert, Esquire [of Roath]
1651	George Bowen, Esquire [of Kittle Hill, Chcriton]
1652	Rees Powell, Esquire [of Coytrahen]
1653	Edward Stradling, Esquire [of Roath]
1654	Edward Dodington, Esquire [of Neath Abbey] *(excused)*
1654	Humphrey Wyndham, Esquire [of Dunraven]
1655	William Bassett [of Miskin]

1656   Richard Lougher, Esquire [of Tythegston]
1657   William Herbert, Esquire [of Swansea]
1658   Stephen Edwards, Esquire [of Stembridge]
1659   Richard David (or Davies), Esquire [of Penmaen, Gower]
1660   Richard David (or Davies), Esquire [of Penmaen, Gower] (*continued in office*)
1661   Herbert Evans, Esquire [of Gnoll, Neath]
1662   Gabriel Lewis, Esquire [of Llanishen]
1663   Edward Gamage [of Newcastle]
1664   John Greenuffe [of Van, Caerphilly, and Bedwas, Monmouthshire]
1665   Edmund Thomas [of Wenvoe Castle]
1666   Martin Button, Esquire [of Duffryn, St Nicholas]
1667   Edward Mathew, Esquire [of Rhoose, and Aberdare]
1668   Thomas Mathew, Esquire [of Castell-y-Mynach, Pentyrch]
1669   Thomas Button, Esquire [of Cottrell, St Nicholas]
1670   Philip Hoby, Esquire [of Neath Abbey]
1671   Edward Thomas, Esquire, of Moulton, [Llancarfan]
1672   Philip Jones, Esquire, of Fonmon Castle
1673   Thomas Powell, Esquire, of Coytrahen
1674   Thomas Lewis, Esquire, of Penmark [Place]
1675   William Thomas, Esquire, of Llanbradach
1676   Richard Seys, Esquire [of Rhyddings, Neath]
1677   Miles Mathew, Esquire, of Llancaiach
1678   Bussy Mansel, Esquire [of Briton Ferry]
1679   Thomas Gibbon, Esquire [of Trecastle, Llanharry]
1680   George Bowen, Esquire [of Kittle Hill, Cheriton]
1681   William Jenkins, Esquire, of Newbridge (*excused*)
1681   Thomas Morgan, Esquire [of Llanrumney]
1682   Thomas Lewis, Esquire [of Llanishen]
1683   Oliver Jones, Esquire [of Fonmon Castle]
1684   Thomas Rees, Esquire (*excused*)
1684   Reynold Deere, Esquire [of Wenvoe]
1685   David Jenkins, Esquire, of Hensol
1686   Sir John Aubrey, Knight [of Llantrithyd]
1687   William Aubrey, Esquire [of Pencoed, Llaniltern]
1688   Sir Humphrey Edwin, Knight [of Llanmihangel] (*excused*)
1688   Sir Edward Mansel, Baronet [of Margam]
1688   William Wogan, Esquire (*listed, but in error. Appointed for Pembrokeshire, but then superseded*)
1689   Thomas Lewis of Penmark [Place] (*excused*)
1689   David Evans, Esquire [of Gwernllwynchwith, Llansamlet, and Gnoll, Neath] (*excused*)
1689   Sir Charles Kemeys, Baronet [of Cefn Mably] (*excused*)
1689   David Evans, Esquire [of Gwernllwynchwith, Llansamlet, and Gnoll, Neath] (*excused*)
1689   Thomas Lewis, Esquire, of Penmark [Place] (*died in office*)

1690	Thomas Carne, Esquire, of Nash [Manor]
1691	John Price, Esquire, of Gellihir [Ilston]
1692	William Seys, Esquire, of Swansea
1693	Robert Carleton, Esquire (*excused*)
1693	Richard Lougher, Esquire, of Tythegston (*excused*)
1693	William Mathew, Esquire, of Aberaman, [Aberdare]
1694	Richard Herbert, Esquire [of Plas Cilybebyll]
1695	John Bennet, Esquire [of Kittle Hill, Cheriton]
1696	Richard Lougher, Esquire [of Tythegston]
1697	Richard Morgan, Esquire [of St George's, Somerset]
1698	George Howell, Esquire, of Bovehill, [St Andrew's Major]
1699	John Whitwich, Esquire, of Marlston, [Berkshire] (*died in office*)
1700	Sir John Thomas, Knight and Baronet [of Wenvoe Castle]
1701	Thomas Mansel, Esquire, of Penrice [Castle]
1702	Oliver St John, Esquire (*excused*)
1702	Daniel Morris, Esquire [of Clun-y-Castell, Resolven]
1703	William Bassett, Esquire [of Cowbridge]
1704	Sir Humphrey Edwin, Knight [of Llanmihangel] (*excused*)
1704	Robert Jones, Esquire [of Fonmon Castle]
1705	Thomas Thomas, Esquire [of Llanbradach]
1706	William Stanley, Esquire [of Neath Abbey]
1707	Roger Powell, Esquire [of Energlyn, Caerphilly]
1708	Richard Carne, Esquire [of Ewenny]
1709	Thomas Button, Esquire [of Cottrell, St Nicholas]
1710	Sir Edward Stradling, Baronet [of St Donat's Castle]
1711	Sir John Aubrey, Baronet [of Llantrithyd]
1712	John Curre, Esquire [of Clemenston]
1713	Sir Charles Kemeys, Baronet [of Cefn Mably]
1714	Hoby Compton, Esquire [of Neath Abbey]
1715	Gabriel Lewis, Esquire [of Llanishen]
1716	Evan Seys, Esquire (*excused*)
1716	John Jones, Esquire [of Duffryn, Aberdare]
1717	Edward Thomas, Esquire, of Ogmore
1718	Thomas Popkin, Esquire [of Fforest, Llansamlet]
1719	Michael Williams, Esquire, of Newcastle, [Bridgend]
1720	William Dawkin, Esquire, of Kilvrough, [Pennard, Gower]
1721	William Richards, Esquire, of Cardiff
1722	William Morgan, Esquire, of Coedygoras, [Llanedeyrn]
1723	Edward Evans, Esquire, of Eaglesbush
1724	James Williams, Esquire, of Cardiff
1725	Charles Edwin, Esquire, of Llanmihangel (*excused*)
1725	Abraham Barbour, Esquire, of St George's[-super-Ely]
1726	Morgan Morgan, Esquire, of Llanrumney
1727	Francis Popham, Esquire (*excused*)
1727	Martin Button, Esquire, of Duffryn, [St Nicholas]
1728	James Thomas, Esquire, of Llanbradach

1729	Robert Jones, Esquire, of Fonmon Castle
1730	John Llewellin, Esquire, of Ynysygerwn
1731	John Carne, Esquire, of Nash [Manor]
1732	Reynold Deere, Esquire [of Penllyn Court]
1733	Herbert Mackworth, Esquire, of Gnoll, [Neath]
1734	William Bassett, Esquire, of Miskin
1735	Grant Gibbon, Esquire [of Trecastle, Llanharry]
1736	Hopkin Rees, Esquire, of St Mary Hill
1737	Robert Knight, Esquire [of Tythegston]
1738	Edmund Lloyd, Esquire, of Cardiff
1739	Thomas Price, Esquire, of Penllergare
1740	Richard Turbervill, Esquire, of Ewenny
1741	Rowland Dawkin, Esquire, of Kilvrough, [Pennard, Gower]
1742	Edward Popham, Esquire, of Merthyr Dyfan (*excused*)
1742	Robert Morris, Esquire, of Ynysarwed
1743	Matthew Deere, Esquire, of Ash Hall, [Welsh St Donat's]
1744	Henry Lucas, Esquire, of Stouthall, [Reynoldston]
1745	Thomas Lewis, Esquire, of Llanishen
1746	Whitlock Nicholl, Esquire, of The Ham, [Llantwit Major]
1747	Thomas Powell, Esquire, of Tondu
1748	John Mathew, Esquire, of Brynchwith, [Llandyfodwg]
1749	Joseph Pryce, Esquire, of Gellihir, [Ilston]
1750	Richard Jenkins, Esquire, of Marlas, [Pyle]
1751	William Evans, Esquire, of Eaglesbush
1752	Rowland Bevan, Esquire, of Oxwich
1753	Thomas Rous, Esquire
1754	Edward Walters, Esquire, of Pitcot, [St Bride's Major]
1755	Thomas Popkin, Esquire [of Fforest, Llansamlet]
1756	Henry Streatfeild, Esquire, of Coity [Castle] (*excused*)
1756	William Bruce, Esquire, of Llanblethian
1757	Thomas Lewis, Esquire, of Newhouse, [Llanishen]
1758	Edward Mathew, Esquire, of Aberaman, [Aberdare]
1759	Thomas Pryce, Esquire, of Duffryn, [St Nicholas]
1760	Sir John de la Fountain Tyrwhitt, Baronet, of St Donat's [Castle]
1761	Samuel Price, Esquire, of Coity
1762	Philip Williams, Esquire, of Dyffryn, [Neath]
1763	Robert Morris, Esquire, of Swansea
1764	Abraham Williams, Esquire, of Cathays, [Cardiff]
1765	Calvert Richard Jones, Esquire, of Swansea
1766	William Curre, Esquire, of Clemenston
1767	Edward Powell, Esquire, of Tondu
1768	Thomas Bennet, Esquire, of Laleston
1769	Thomas Mathew, Esquire, of Llandaff [Court]
1770	Richard Gorton, Esquire, of Burry's Green, [Gower]
1771	William Thomas, Esquire, of Llanblethian
1772	Edward Thomas, Esquire, of Tregroes, [Coychurch]

1773	William Dawkin, Esquire, of Kilvrough, [Pennard]
1774	John Edmondes, Esquire, of Cowbridge
1775	Daniel Jones, Esquire, of Glanbran
1776	William Hurst, Esquire, of Gabalfa
1777	David Thomas, Esquire, of Pwllywrach, [Colwinston]
1778	John Lucas, Esquire, of Stouthall, [Reynoldston]
1779	Bartholomew Greenwood, Esquire, of Cardiff (*excused, being Bailiff of Cardiff*)
1779	Christopher Bassett, Esquire, of Lanelay
1780	Peter Birt, Esquire, of Wenvoe Castle
1781	Charles Bowen, Esquire, of Merthyr Mawr
1782	Thomas Mansel Talbot, Esquire, of Margam
1783	William Kemeys, Esquire, of Ynysarwed
1784	John Richards, Esquire, of Energlyn, [Caerphilly]
1785	Stephen White, Esquire, of Miskin
1786	Thomas Drake Tyrwhitt, Esquire, of St Donat's Castle
1787	John Price, Esquire, of Llandaff Court
1788	Richard Jenkins, Esquire, of Pantynawel, [Llangeinor]
1789	John Llewellin, Esquire, of [Great House], Welsh St Donat's
1790	William Lewis, Esquire, of Greenmeadow, [Pentyrch]
1791	John Richards, Esquire, of Corner House, [1 St Mary Street], Cardiff
1792	John Llewelyn, Esquire, of Ynysygerwn
1793	John Lucas, Esquire, of Stouthall, [Reynoldston]
1794	John Kemeys-Tynte, Esquire, of Cefn Mably (*excused*)
1794	Henry Knight, Esquire, of Tythegston
1795	Wyndham Lewis, Esquire, of Llanishen
1796	Herbert Hurst, Esquire, of Gabalfa
1797	Robert Rous, Esquire, of Cwrtyrala, [Michaelston-le-Pit]
1798	Samuel Richardson, Esquire, of Hensol [Castle]
1799	John Goodrich, Esquire, of Energlyn, [Caerphilly]
1800	Robert Jenner, Esquire, of Wenvoe Castle
1801	Llewelyn Traherne, Esquire, of St Hilary (*excused*)
1801	Robert Jones, Esquire, of Fonmon Castle
1802	Richard Mansel Phillips, Esquire, of Sketty Hall, [Swansea]
1803	John Morris, Esquire, of Clasemont
1804	Richard Turbervill Picton, Esquire, of Ewenny
1804	Richard Turbervill Turbervill, Esquire, of Ewenny
1805	Thomas Markham, Esquire, of Nash [Manor]
1806	Anthony Bacon, Esquire, of Cyfarthfa, [Merthyr Tydfil]
1807	George Winch, Esquire, of Clemenston
1808	The Hon. William Booth Grey, of Duffryn, [St Nicholas] (*excused*)
1808	Richard Nathaniel Miers, Esquire, of Cadoxton-juxta-Neath
1809	Jeremiah Homfray, Esquire, of Llandaff [House]
1810	Thomas Lockwood, Esquire, of Dan-y-Graig, [Swansea]
1811	Sir Robert Lynch Blosse, Baronet, of Gabalfa
1812	Morgan Popkin Traherne, Esquire, of Coytrahen

1813   William Jones, Esquire, of Corntown [Lodge, Ewenny]
1814   The Hon. William Booth Grey, of Duffryn, [St Nicholas]
1815   William Tait, Esquire, of Cardiff (*died in office*)
1816   Henry John Grant, Esquire, of Gnoll, Neath (*excused*)
1816   Richard John Hill, Esquire, of Plymouth Lodge, [Merthyr Tydfil]
1817   Thomas Bates Rous, Esquire, of Cwrtyrala, [Michaelston-le-Pit]
1818   Lewis Weston Dillwyn, Esquire, of Penllergare
1819   Josiah John Guest, Esquire, of Dowlais [House, Merthyr Tydfil]
1820   Richard Blakemore, Esquire, of Velindra, [Whitchurch]
1821   William Forman, Esquire, of Penydarren, [Merthyr Tydfil]
1822   Sir John Morris, Baronet, of Bryn, [and Sketty Park, Swansea]
1823   John Edwards, Esquire, of Rheola
1824   John Bassett, Esquire, of Bonvilston House
1825   John Bennet, Esquire, of Laleston
1826   Thomas Edward Thomas, Esquire, of Swansea
1827   John Henry Vivian, Esquire, of Marino, [Swansea]
1828   Robert Francis Jenner, Esquire, of Wenvoe Castle
1829   William Crawshay the younger, Esquire, of Cyfarthfa Castle, Merthyr Tydfil
1830   William Williams, Esquire, of Aberpergwm
1831   Richard Hoare Jenkins, Esquire, of Llanharan House
1832   Frederick Fredericks, Esquire, of Dyffryn, [Neath]
1833   Richard Turbervill, Esquire, of Ewenny
1834   Henry John Grant, Esquire, of Gnoll, [Neath]
1835   John Dillwyn Llewelyn, Esquire, of Penllergare
1836   Thomas Penrice, Esquire, of Kilvrough, [Pennard, Gower]
1837   Howel Gwyn, Esquire, of Alltwen
1838   Nash Vaughan Edwards Vaughan, Esquire, of Lanelay (*excused*)
1838   Howel Gwyn, Esquire, of Alltwen (*excused*)
1838   Robert Oliver Jones, Esquire, of Fonmon Castle
1839   Charles Henry Smith, Esquire, of Gwernllwynchwith, [Llansamlet]
1840   Michael Williams, Esquire, of Morfa, [Swansea, and of Caerhays Castle, Cornwall]
1841   Joseph Martin, Esquire, of Ynystawe
1842   Henry Lucas, Esquire, of Uplands, [Swansea]
1843   John Homfray, Esquire, of Llandaff House
1844   John Bruce Pryce, Esquire, of Duffryn, [St Nicholas, and Duffryn, Aberdare]
1845   Robert Savours, Esquire, of Trecastle, [Llanharry]
1846   Richard Franklen, Esquire, of Clemenston
1847   Nash Vaughan Edwards Vaughan, Esquire, of Rheola
1848   Thomas William Booker, Esquire, of Velindra, [Whitchurch]
1849   Robert Boteler, Esquire, of Llandough[-juxta-Cowbridge] Castle, and Maesmawr, [Llantwit Fardre]
1850   Rowland Fothergill, Esquire, of Hensol Castle
1851   Gervase Powell Turbervill, Esquire, of Ewenny
1852   Griffith Llewellyn, Esquire, of Baglan Hall

1853   Richard Hill Miers, Esquire, of Ynyspenllwch
1854   William Llewellyn, Esquire, of Court Colman
1855   Wyndham William Lewis, Esquire, of The Heath, Cardiff
1856   John Samuel, Esquire, of Newton House, [Welsh St Donat's]
1857   Evan Williams, Esquire, of Dyffrynffrwd
1858   Henry Lewis, Esquire, of Greenmeadow, [Pentyrch]
1859   Charles Crofts Williams, Esquire, of Roath Court
1860   George Grey Rous, Esquire, of Cwrtyrala, [Michaelston-le-Pit]
1861   Edward Robert Wood, Esquire, of Stouthall, [Reynoldston]
1862   Sir Ivor Bertie Guest, Baronet, of Sully House
1863   John Popkin Traherne, Esquire, of Coytrahen
1864   Robert Francis Lascelles Jenner, Esquire, of Wenvoe Castle
1865   Thomas William Booker, Esquire, of Velindra, [Whitchurch]
1866   William Graham Vivian, Esquire, of Singleton, [Swansea]
1867   Thomas Penrice, Esquire, of Kilvrough House, [Pennard, Gower]
1868   George Thomas Clark, Esquire, of Talygarn, [Pontyclun]
1869   Edward Romilly, Esquire, of Porthkerry
1870   George William Griffiths Thomas, Esquire, of Coedriglan, [and Llanbradach]
1871   Vaughan Hanning Lee, Esquire, of Lanelay
1872   Charles Henry Williams, Esquire, of Roath Court
1873   Francis Edmund Stacey, Esquire, of Llandough-juxta-Cowbridge [Castle]
1874   John Whitlock Nicholl Carne, Esquire, DCL, of St Donat's Castle
1875   Morgan Stuart Williams, Esquire, of Aberpergwm
1876   Thomas Picton Turbervill, Esquire, of Ewenny
1877   Herbert Lloyd, Esquire, of Plas Cilybebyll
1878   John Talbot Dillwyn Llewelyn, Esquire, of Ynysygerwn
1879   Richard Knight Prichard, Esquire, of Graig Avon, Taibach
1880   John Trevillian Jenkin, Esquire, of The Mirador, Swansea
1881   John Crow Richardson, Esquire, of Pant-y-Gwydir, Swansea
1882   Sir Joseph Layton Elmes Spearman, Baronet, of Lanelay Hall
1883   Lieutenant-General Henry Roxley Benson, CB, of Fairy Hill, [Gower]
1884   John Cole Nicholl, Esquire, of Merthyr Mawr
1885   Lieutenant-Colonel Edward Stock Hill, CB, of Rookwood, Llandaff
1886   Lieutenant-Colonel Charles Richard Franklen of Clemenston
1887   Tudor Crawshay, Esquire, of Bonvilston House
1888   John Henry Rowland, Esquire, of Ffrwd Vale, Neath
1889   Sir John Jones Jenkins, Knight, of The Grange, Swansea
1890   Frederick Lewis Davis, Esquire, of Bryndderwen, Ferndale
1891   Edward Rice Daniel, Esquire, of Cwmgelly, Swansea
1892   Arthur Gilbertson, Esquire, of Glanrhyd, Pontardawe
1893   Robert Forrest, Esquire, of [Greenwood], St Fagans
1894   Morgan Bransby Williams, Esquire, of Killay
1895   Ralph Thurstan Bassett, Esquire, of Crossways, Cowbridge
1896   Colonel John Picton Turbervill of Ewenny
1897   Godfrey Lewis Clark, Esquire, of Talygarn, Pontyclun

1898   Thomas Roe Thompson, Esquire, of Erw'r Delyn, Penarth
1899   John Iltyd Dillwyn Nicholl, Esquire, of Merthyr Mawr
1900   Sir Robert Armine Morris, Baronet, of Sketty Park, Swansea
1901   Griffith Thomas, Esquire, of Court Herbert, Neath
1902   Edward Daniel, Esquire, of Rose Hill, Swansea
1903   John Glasbrook, Esquire, of Sketty Court, Swansea
1904   William Walters, Esquire, of Ffynone, Swansea
1905   Herbert Eccles, Esquire, of Penrhiwtyn House, Neath
1906   William Henry Edwards, Esquire, of The Poplars, Morriston
1907   Walter Rice Evans, Esquire, of Eaglesbush
1908   Frederick William Gibbins, Esquire, of Garthmor, Neath
1909   David Lewis, Esquire, of Gorseinon [and Sunnybank, Mumbles]
1910   William John Percy Player, Esquire, of The Quarr, Clydach
1911   William James Tatem, Esquire, of The Court, St Fagans
1912   Colonel William Charles Wright of Gwern Einon, Blackpill
1913   James Herbert Cory, Esquire, of Coryton, [Whitchurch]
1914   Thomas Jeremiah Davies, Esquire, of Morfydd House, Morriston
1915   Trevor Stanley Jones, Esquire, of Frondeg, Radyr
1916   Sir John Wesley Courtis, Knight, of Fairwater Croft, Llandaff
1917   Daniel Radcliffe, Esquire, of Tal-y-Werydd, Cardiff
1918   John Arthur Jones, Esquire, of Ty Dyfrig, Llandaff
1919   Edmund Lyons Evan-Thomas, Esquire, of [Gnoll], Neath, and 13 Bramham Gardens, London, SW5
1920   Henry Gethin Lewis, Esquire, of Porthkerry Rectory
1921   Wyndham Damer Clark, Esquire, of Talygarn, Pontyclun
1922   Sir Francis Caradoc Rose-Price, Baronet, of Hensol Castle
1923   Sidney Hutchinson Byass, Esquire, of Llandough[-juxta-Cowbridge] Castle
1924   Wyndham Ivor Radcliffe, Esquire, of Druidstone, [St Mellon's, Monmouthshire]
1925   William Herbert Clydwin Llewellyn, Esquire, of Court Colman
1926   Admiral Algernon Walker-Heneage-Vivian, CB, MVO, of Clyne [Castle, Swansea]
1927   David George Hall, Esquire, of Gwentland, Marine Parade, Penarth
1928   Theodore Gibbins, Esquire, of Glynfelin, Neath
1929   William Simons, Esquire, of Penylan Court, Cardiff
1930   Major Evan John Carne David of Fairwater House, Cardiff
1931   Sir Lewis Lougher, Knight, of [Dan-y-Bryn], Radyr
1932   Major Sir William Cope, Baronet, TD, of Cornborough, Porthcawl
1933   Thomas Edward Morel, Esquire, of Roxburgh, Penarth
1934   Henry Herbert Merrett, Esquire, of Bryn Hafod, Llandaff
1935   John Herbert Cory, Esquire, of The Grange, St Bride's-super-Ely
1936   Sir William James Thomas, Baronet, of Birchwood Grange, Penylan, Cardiff
1937   Captain John Elliot Seager, MC, of Ty Gwyn Court, Penylan, Cardiff
1938   Sir Emsley Carr, Knight, of Wonford, Walton Heath, Tadworth, Surrey
1939   William John Treseder Treseder-Griffin, Esquire, of Lisvane House,

	Lisvane, Cardiff
1940	Harry Lascelles Carr, Esquire, of Corbar, Beach Hill, Hadley Wood, Barnet, Hertfordshire
1941	Major Joseph Gerald Gaskell, TD, of Cwrt Cefn, Lisvane
1942	Reginald Pendrill St John Charles, Esquire, of Newton House, Porthcawl
1943	Major David Percy Davies of Charnwood, Radlett, Hertfordshire
1944	Selwyn Rawlings Martyn, Esquire, of The Mount, Dinas Powis
1945	Jonah Arnold, Esquire, OBE, of Tower House, Lougher Gardens, Porthcawl
1946	Sir Willie Reardon-Smith, Baronet, of Golding, Peterston-super-Ely
1947	Colonel Robert Godfrey Llewellyn, CBE, MC, TD, of Tredilion Park, Abergavenny, Monmouthshire
1948	Edward Julian Pode, Esquire, of Great House, Bonvilston
1949	Sir Percy Edward Thomas, Knight, OBE, of Tregenna, Mill Road, Llanishen
1950	Lieutenant-Colonel Sir Rhys Llewellyn, Baronet, of The Court, St Fagans
1951	David Martyn Evans Bevan, Esquire, of Twyn-yr-Hydd, Margam
1952	Major Douglas Alexander Duncan of Innisfree, Clinton Road, Penarth
1953	Sir Hugo Robert Brooke Boothby, Baronet, of Fonmon Castle
1954	Llewellyn Ward, Esquire, of Highways, St Andrews Road, Dinas Powis
1955	Charles Reginald Wheeler, Esquire, CBE, of Highfield, Bradford Place, Penarth
1956	Major Edmund Ashley Charles Westby, TD, of Trehedyn, Peterston-super-Ely
1957	Group-Captain Ronald Scott Sugden, CBE, AFC, of Merevale, Dinas Powis
1958	Squadron-Leader Henry Gethin Lewis, RAFVR, of Cliffside, Penarth
1959	John Cory, Esquire, of The Grange, St Bride's-super-Ely
1960	Duncan Hubert David Alexander, Esquire, OBE, TD, of Star House, Capel Llaniltern
1961	William Frederick Cartwright, Esquire, of Castle-upon-Alun, St Bride's Major
1962	The Hon. Anthony George Berry of Llantrithyd House, Llantrithyd
1963	David Wymar Vaughan, Esquire, CBE, of Colwinston House, Colwinston
1964	Christopher Gordon Llewellin Cory, Esquire, of Penllyn Castle
1965	Richard Charles Quintin Picton-Turbervill, Esquire, of Ewenny Priory
1966	George Mervyn Williams, Esquire, MC, TD, of Llanharan House, Llanharan
1967	Jim Stanley Hamilton Mathews, [Esquire], of West House, Llantwit Major
1968	Mrs Susan Eva Williams, MBE, of Caercady, Welsh St Donat's
1969	Lieutenant-Colonel John Rhodri Llewellyn Traherne of Castellau, Llantrisant
1970	Arthur Geoffrey Gilbertson, Esquire, of Brynfro, Llanblethian
1971	Christopher Paul Mansel Methuen-Campbell, Esquire, of Penrice Castle, Oxwich, Swansea
1972	George Forbes Raymond Hayes, Esquire, of Brocastle, Bridgend
1973	Mathew Caradoc Thomas Prichard, Esquire, of Pwllywrach, Cowbridge

Sheriffs of the County of Mid Glamorgan
1974–1994

(Descriptions are given as on the document of appointment)

1974 John Lewis Maybery Bevan, Esquire, TD,
      of Croffta, Groes-Faen, Pontyclun, Llantrisant

1975 Sir (Herbert) Leslie Joseph,
      of Coedargraig, Newton, Porthcawl

1976 Douglas George Badham, Esquire, CBE, JP, DL,
      of Plas Watford, Caerphilly

1977 Douglas Andrew Scott, Esquire, OBE, JP,
      of Windyridge, 4 Locks Lane, Porthcawl

1978 Murray Adams McLaggan, Esquire, JP, MA,
      of Merthyr Mawr House

1979 Major George Morgan Thomas Lindsay,
      of Glanmor, Southerndown

1980 Robert Watkin Stacey Knight, Esquire, DL,
      of Tynycaeau, St Bride's Major

1981 Edward Arthur Lewis, Esquire, CStJ, JP, BA,
      of Grove House, 38 Lan Park Road, Pontypridd

1982 William Kingdon Eynon, Esquire,
      of Tusker House, Newton, Porthcawl

1983   Alan Edward Mayer, Esquire,
      of Tŷ Mawr, Efail Isaf, Pontypridd

1984   Edward Rea, Esquire,
      of Llechwedd, 8 Y Parc, Groes Faen, Pontyclun

1985   Owain Anthony Mervyn Williams, Esquire,
      of Llanharan House, Llanharan

1986   Mrs Kathrin Elizabeth Thomas, JP,
      of Gelli Hir, Nelson

1987   Peter Dobson Allen, Esquire,
      of Furzebrook, 82 Merthyr Mawr Road, Bridgend

1988   Derek William Charles Morgan, Esquire,
      of Erw Graig, Merthyr Mawr

1989   Harold John Tamplin, Esquire, OBE,
      of Cwmnofydd Farm, Machen

1990   Islwyn Thomas Rees, Esquire,
      of Tan-y-Lan Farm, St Mary Hill

1991   Lieutenant-Colonel David Edward Cox, LVO, MBE,
      of Trem-y-Mor, 221 West Road, Nottage, Porthcawl

1992   Kenneth Merlin David Johns, Esquire, OBE,
      of Pencoed House, Capel Llaniltern

1993   Mrs Barbara Magdalene Ladbrooke
      of Longacre Farm, Coity

In November of each year three names from each county are sent forward for submission to the Sovereign. It has become customary for the first name on the list to be pricked with a bodkin in accordance with tradition. The sheriff appointed for Mid Glamorgan, taking office in March 1994 is

1994   Colonel Thomas Udy Buckthought, TD, DL,
      of The Bucks, 13 Underwood, Caerphilly

Sheriffs of the County of South Glamorgan 1974–1994

(Descriptions are given as on the document of appointment)

1974 Colonel George Frederick Kenneth Morgan, MC, TD, DL,
    of Llantrithyd House, Llantrithyd

1975 Anthony Selwyn Martyn, Esquire, JP,
    of Tinkinswood, St Nicholas

1976 Joseph Gerald Gaskell, Esquire, TD,
    of Bryn Robin, Michaelston-le-Pit

1977 Francis Edward Sutherland Hayes, Esquire,
    of Llansannor House, Llansannor

1978 Christopher Michael Brain, Esquire,
    of Trelawne, Peterston-super-Ely

1979 Harold Emmott Williams, Esquire,
    of 6 Augusta Road, Penarth

1980 Henry Gethin Lewis, junior, Esquire, JP,
    of The Old Rectory, Porthkerry

1981 Colonel Christopher Matthew Peterson, TD, JP, DL,
    of 15 Llandennis Avenue, Cyncoed, Cardiff

1982 Ivan Dale Owen, Esquire,
    of Cliff House, Cliff Walk, Penarth

1983   Ian Eric Colston, Esquire, MA, FRICS,
        of Boverton House, Boverton, Llantwit Major

1984   Cecil Herbert Rapport, Esquire, MBE, JP,
        of Hollybush House, Hollybush Road, Cyncoed, Cardiff

1985   William Emrys Evans, Esquire, CBE,
        of Maesglas, Pen-y-turnpike, Dinas Powis

1986   Brooke Charles Boothby, Esquire,
        of Fonmon Castle

1987   Sir Donald Walters, Knight,
        of 120 Cyncoed Road, Cardiff

1988   Dudley Henry Fisher, Esquire,
        of 8 Cyncoed Avenue, Cardiff

1989   Christopher Leslie Pollard, Esquire,
        of Penarth House, Penarth

1990   Brian Keith Thomas, Esquire,
        of 17 Millwood, Lisvane

1991   Michael John Clay, Esquire,
        of Llwynhelig, Cowbridge

1992   Alastair Owen Golley, Esquire,
        of Little Westra, Dinas Powys

1993   Commander John Mascall Darby Curteis, RNR,
        of Clive House, St Fagans

In November of each year three names from each county are sent forward for submission to the Sovereign. It has become customary for the first name on the list to be pricked with a bodkin in accordance with tradition. The sheriff appointed for South Glamorgan, taking office in April 1994, is

1994   Mrs Joanna Gethin Cory, JP
        of Penllyn Castle, Cowbridge

Mrs Cory is the widow of the sheriff of Glamorgan for 1964, and the sister, daughter and granddaughter of the sheriffs of 1980 (South Glamorgan), 1958 and 1920 respectively. She is the sister-in-law, daughter-in-law and great-niece-in-law of the sheriffs of 1959, 1935 and 1913.

Sheriffs of the County of West Glamorgan
1974–1994

(Descriptions are given as on the document of appointment)

1974   Alan Burnyeat Turnbull, Esquire,
          of Home Farm, Penrice

1975   Claud Gerald Bellingham, Esquire,
          of The Meadows, Bishopston

1976   Martin Thomas, Esquire,
          of Cae Glas, 102 Wern Road, Skewen

1977   Captain Robert Cameron Hastie, RD, ADC, DL, RNR,
          of Upper Hareslade, Bishopston

1978   Donald Humphrey Davies, Esquire,
          of Highways, Hill Grove, Caswell, Swansea

1979   Keith Cyril Austin Bailey, Esquire,
          of Ailsa Craig, Caswell Bay, Swansea

1980   Colonel Michael Rowland Godfrey Llewellyn,
          of Glebe House, Penmaen

1981   Alexander Herbert Lindsey Eccles, Esquire,
          of Bryn Cottage, Penmaen

1982   Arthur Gordon Chilcott, Esquire,
          of Whyteholme, Caswell Road, Mumbles, Swansea

1983   David Hunter Andrews, Esquire,
        of Cefn Bryn House, Penmaen

1984   Brian Brendan Hickey, Esquire, TD,
        of Llys Meddyg, 3 Llwynderw Drive, Blackpill, Swansea

1985   Edward Gwynne Thomas, Esquire,
        of 1 Caswell Avenue, Mumbles, Swansea

1986   Eden Martin Hughes Evans, Esquire,
        of Broadoak House, Loughor

1987   Philip Richard Vernon Watkins, Esquire,
        of Beaufort Lodge, 31 Caswell Road, Mumbles, Swansea

1988   Dr Stuart Poole Jenkins,
        of North Croft, North Lodge Close, Penllergaer

1989   Dr Brian Kay Davison,
        of 22 Whitegates, Mayals, Swansea

1990   John Brian Dickenson Simpson, Esquire,
        of 18 Wychwood Close, Langland, Swansea

1991   Dr Edward Morgan Roberts,
        of 7 Ten Acre Wood, Margam

1992   William Isaac James, Esquire, MBE,
        of Hafod, Llanrhidian

1993   Alan Charles Frederick Aylesbury, Esquire, OBE,
        of 28 Rhyd yr Helyg, Sketty, Swansea

In November of each year three names from each county are sent forward for submission to the Sovereign. It has become customary for the first name on the list to be pricked with a bodkin in accordance with tradition. The sheriff appointed for West Glamorgan, taking office in April 1994, is

1994   Colin Reginald Rees, Esquire
        of 65 West Cross Lane, West Cross, Swansea

The Office of Under Sheriff
List of Under Sheriffs 1541–1994

The Office of Under Sheriff

by
John Otto-Jones
MA (Oxon.), BA (Wales)
Under Sheriff of Glamorgan

The area for which an under sheriff acts is referred to as a bailiwick. Prior to 1 April 1974, there was a single bailiwick of Glamorgan although one area of the bailiwick was the subject of separate administration. This area consisted of the land within the old county lying to the west of a line running approximately from Ystalyfera through Clydach and Jersey Marine and to the west. The area was known as the Liberties of Gower and Kilvey and was the subject of a grant by King James I to Edward, Earl of Worcester, and his heirs. Certain High Court writs within these Liberties were administered by the Bailiff of the Liberties appointed from time to time by the Duke of Beaufort. This arrangement ceased on 31 March 1974 on the creation of the current bailiwicks of Glamorgan and Swansea.

The establishment of the new counties by virtue of the Local Government Act 1972 included the creation of three new counties, namely Mid Glamorgan, South Glamorgan and West Glamorgan, in place of the former county of Glamorgan, to take effect from 1 April 1974.

In 1974 the Lord Chancellor, by virtue of the Under Sheriffs' Bailiwick Order 1974, ordered that as from 1 April 1974 the area for which the under sheriff of Glamorgan acted immediately before that date should become two separate bailiwicks to be known as the bailiwick of Glamorgan and the bailiwick of Swansea, such bailiwicks to comprise the following areas:

Bailiwick	Areas comprised in bailiwick
Glamorgan	The county of Mid Glamorgan except the areas formerly in the administrative counties of Brecon and Monmouthshire.
	The county of South Glamorgan except the area formerly in the administrative county of Monmouthshire.
	In the county of West Glamorgan the districts of Afan and Neath.

106

Swansea   In the county of West Glamorgan the districts of Lliw Valley and Swansea.

The sheriff is required by statute to appoint an under sheriff in writing, and a copy of such appointment must be lodged with the proper officer of the appropriate county council to be filed among the county records.

The under sheriff acts in the name of the sheriff who is therefore responsible for the acts and omissions of the under sheriff. The under sheriff operates as the deputy of the sheriff in carrying out any of the functions of the sheriff except the function as returning officer at parliamentary elections. If the sheriff should die during his year of office, the Sheriffs' Act 1887 requires the under sheriff to exercise the office of sheriff in the name of the deceased sheriff until another sheriff has been appointed and has made his declaration of office.

One of the main duties carried out by the under sheriff on behalf of the sheriff is the execution of High Court writs within the county. These include writs of *fieri facias* (relating to recovery of money), writs of possession (recovery of land) and writs of delivery (recovery of chattels). For these purposes sheriff's officers are appointed who report regularly to the under sheriff. The payment of rewards issued from time to time by the judiciary is also the primary responsibility of the sheriff subject to reimbursement by the Lord Chancellor's Department. This operation is carried out by the under sheriff in the name of the high sheriff. Generally the under sheriff is involved, with others, in the organization of the attendances of high sheriffs at Crown Courts and the arrangements for the inauguration ceremonies which take place at the commencement of each shrieval year, together with the cathedral services which are held in October at the commencement of each legal year.

Under Sheriffs of the County of Glamorgan
1541–1974
1974–1994

In the earlier years of this list the under sheriff was often a relation of the sheriff, or someone within his political faction, who would enjoy the benefit of the customary profits of the office. In times when it was usual for favours to be accorded in expectation of an appropriate return, the office of under sheriff might well have yielded even further opportunities of gain, for example, a gift made in gratitude for keeping a name off the jury list.

In contrast, by the end of the eighteenth century, the duties of under sheriff were being undertaken increasingly by prominent attorneys (precursors of the solicitors who hold that office today), although it was sometimes a clerk in a practice who carried out the duties. In particular the partnership of John Wood (father and son) and William Vaughan occupied the office through a period of several years.

The list which follows is based on several manuscript compilations (between which there are some variations) held by the Glamorgan Record Office, Cardiff, and the West Glamorgan County Archive Service, Swansea. Some of these compilations date the shrieval year given in this list from the year of appointment, which, before the mid-eighteenth century, was in the previous November or December.

1541	Jenkin Franklen, Gentleman, of Swansea
1542	William Bassett, Gentleman, of Bewper [Beaupré]
1543	James Button of Worlton
1544	John Turbervill of Llanblethian
1545	Thomas Lewis
1546	William Meyrick
1547	William Jones, Gentleman
1548	Robert Stradling, sheriff's brother

1549	John Smith of Cardiff
1550	Thomas Powell of Langonoyd [Llangynwyd]
1551	James Thomas, sheriff's son
1552	Henry Lewis of Cardiff
1553	David John Vaughan
1554	Thomas Powell of Langonoyd
1555	Miles Button, Esquire
1556	Thomas Griffith
1557	Miles Button, Esquire
1558	Jenkin William of Cowbridge
1559	John Unett
1560	John Smith
1561	Thomas Griffith
1562	John Kemeys of Cefn Mably
1563	Richard Thomas
1564	William Herbert of Cardiff
1565	Robert Button
1566	Edward Holland
1567	John Smith
1568	Henry Mathew, sheriff's brother
1569	Walter Williams
1570	Roger Seys, Gentleman
1571	David Robert of Cardiff
1572	John Smith
1573	Jenkin Williams
1574	Leyson Lewis
1575	Walter Williams of Kellygare [Gelligaer]
1576	Thomas Powell
1577	Reynold David
1578	William Herbert of Cardiff *or* Lewis Griffith
1579	Robert Thomas of Cowbridge
1580	Henry Mathew, sheriff's brother
1581	William David
1582	Lewis Griffith of Cilybebyll
1583	Lambrook Stradling of Cardiff
1584	Rees *or* Robert Lewis
1585	John Andrew
1586	John Gamage
1587	Gabriel Lewis, Esquire, of Llanishen
1588	George Kemeys of Llanblethian
1589	Edward Button, sheriff's son
1590	Morgan Gibbon of St Fagans
1591	Thomas Pranch
1592	Lewis Griffith of Killybebill [Cilybebyll]
1593	Marmaduke Mathew
1594	Anthony Powell

1595	William St John [Knight]
1596	John Stradling, Gentleman
1597	Thomas Bassett, sheriff's son
1598	William Powell
1599	Thomas Lewis Reynold
1600	William Williams
1601	Hopkin Evans, Gentleman
1602	Gabriel Lewis, Esquire
1603	Thomas Bassett, Gentleman
1604	Anthony Powell, Gentleman
1605	Morgan Cradock, Gentleman
1606	Hopkin David Edward
1607	Philip Williams
1608	William Stradling
1609	Thomas Bassett, sheriff's son
1610	William Meyrick, sheriff's brother
1611	David Lloyd of Cardiff
1612	Philip William of Eglwysilan
1613	William Robert of St Andrews [*or* St Athan]
1614	Miles Mathew, sheriff's brother
1615	Evan Thomas ap Evan
1616	Rees Knapp
1617	Henry Penry, Gentleman
1618	Robert Mathew, sheriff's brother
1619	Owen Price, Gentleman
1620	George Williams
1621	William Roberts
1622	Jenkin Craddock, Gentleman, of Llancarfan
1623	John Rowe of Gower
1624	John Powell of Maesteg
1625	Rees Howard of Llantrithyd
1626	Owen Price, *died in office and was succeeded by* William Price
1627	James Thomas, sheriff's brother
1628	Watkin Lougher of Nottage
1629	Jenkin Cradock of Llancarfan
1630	Lewis Thomas Richard *or* Evan Thomas
1631	Lewis Thomas, Gentleman
1632	George Williams
1633	Morgan Griffith
1634	Henry Penry of Llantrithyd
1635	Lewis Thomas Griffith
1636	[?Lewis Thomas of Llangyfelach]
1637	Jenkin Cradock of Llancarfan
1638	Thomas Powell
1639	Morgan Howard
1640	Morgan Griffith

1641	Henry Penry of Llantrithyd
1642	Richard Bevan/ap Evan
1643	Robert William of St Hilary
1644, 1645	Morgan Howard
1646, 1647	Richard ap Evan
1648	Evan Prichard of Deweddid
1649	William Morgan of Neath
1650	John Griffith
1651	John Bowen, sheriff's son
1652	Robert Thomas
1653	Lewis William
1654	Humphrey Wyndham, sheriff's son
1655	Richard ap Evan
1656	Watkin John/Jones, Gentleman, of Monkton, Wick
1657	Thomas David, Gentleman
1658	George Thomas
1659	Leyson Davies, sheriff's brother
1660	John Morgan
1661	David Evans of Neath Abbey
1662	William Morgan of Rupina [Rhiwbina]
1663	John Powell
1664	William Morgan
1665	Edmund Perkins
1666	Moore Perkins
1667	John Richards of Henllan
1668	Miles Mathews of Cardiff, sheriff's uncle
1669	David Thomas of Llysworney
1670	John Llewellin of Ynysygerwn
1671	John Powell
1672	David Evans
1673	Edward Williams of St Mary Church
1674	Moore Perkins
1675	John Thomas of Llancarfan
1676	Rowland Harries of Bryncoch, Neath
1677	Edward Williams of St Mary Church
1678	Jervis/Gervase Powell of Maesteg
1679	Charles Evans/Jevans of Llantwit Fardre
1680	John Powell
1681	William Morgan the younger of Coedygoras
1682	William Morgan the elder of Coedygoras
1683	John Watkins of Gower
1684	Thomas Morgan of Coedygoras
1685	Jervis/Gervase Powell
1686	Evan Edwards
1687	Charles Evans/Jevans
1688	Edward Williams of St Mary Church

1689	Robert Powell of Llysworney
1690	David Thomas of Llysworney
1691	John Watkins of Gower
1692	John Deere, Esquire, of Llantwit [Major]
1693	Charles Evans/Jevans of Llantwit Fardre
1694	Griffith Evans of Gellygron [Llantrisant]
1695	Evan Evans
1696	Edward Thomas of Pwllywrach
1697	Jervis/Gervase Powell of Llantrisant
1698	Richard Bassett of St Andrews
1699	Robert Powell of Llysworney
1700	Charles Evans of Llantwit Fardre
1701	Evan Evans
1702	Jervis/Gervase Powell
1703	William Llewellin of Monkton
1704	Thomas Williams of Llanblethian
1705	Roger Wilkins of Cowbridge
1706	Thomas Hawkins [of Neath]
1707	Michael Richards of Cardiff
1708	Edward Jenkins of Llandough [-juxta-Cowbridge]
1709	Watkin Morgan, clerk to his uncle, Edward Jenkins
1710	Robert Powell of Wilton
1711	Edward Jenkins of Llandough [-juxta-Cowbridge]
1712	Thomas Wilkins of Llanblethian
1713	Evan Evans, clerk to Thomas Wilkins
1714	Thomas Cory of Margam
1715	Gabriel Powell of Swansea
1716	John Jones, sheriff's son
1717	Thomas Cory of Margam
1718	William Frampton, clerk to Gabriel Powell
1719	Anthony Maddocks
1720	William Phillips of Swansea
1721	Michael Richards of Cardiff, sheriff's brother
1722	Henry Morgan, sheriff's brother
1723	Thomas Craddock of Margam
1724	Henry Llewellin of Cardiff
1725	Edward Herbert of Cardiff
1726	Cann Wilkins of Llanblethian
1727	Edward Powell of Brynhill
1728	Henry Llewellin of Cardiff
1729	Richard Powell of Llandow
1730	Gabriel Powell the younger of Swansea
1731	Richard Leyson of Prisk [Welsh St Donat's]
1732	Edward Thomas, sheriff's nephew
1733	William Powell of Swansea
1734	Thomas Leyson of Prisk

1735	Richard Leyson of Prisk
1736	David Lewis of Penkern for Richard Leyson
1737	Anthony Maddocks, *sworn but superseded by*
1737	Richard Powell of Llandow
1738	William Powell of Llanharan [sheriff's brother-in-law]
1739	Hugh Powell of Swansea
1740	Richard Powell of Llandow
1741	Richard Dawkins of Hendrewen, sheriff's cousin
1742	John Jeffreys, Gentleman, of Swansea
1743	Anthony Maddocks of Cefnidfa
1744	Edward Hancorn, Gentleman, of Pitt, Gower
1745	Richard Powell of Llandow
1746	Edward Lewis of Penlline
1747	Edward Savours of Coed Gynllan *or* Coed y cynlle
1748	John Thomas of Cowbridge
1749	John Morgan of Swansea
1750	Anthony Maddocks, Gentleman, of Cefnidfa
1751	Hugh Powell of Swansea
1752	Edward Hancorn, Gentleman
1753	Thomas Edmondes of Cowbridge
1754	Nathaniel Taynton of Cowbridge
1755	Edward Hancorn, Gentleman
1756	John Thomas of Cowbridge
1757	Richard Thomas, clerk to Thomas Edwards of Cardiff
1758	William Humphrey, clerk to John Thomas of Cowbridge
1759	Mansel Williams of Neath
1760	William Rees of St Mary Hill, sheriff's steward
1761	Walter Pruddero, Gentleman, of Llangan, for William Rees
1762	Mansel Williams of Neath, sheriff's brother
1763	Elias Jenkins of Swansea
1764	Thomas Williams of Cowbridge
1765	William Jenkins of Neath
1766	Edward Lewis of Penlline
1767	William Jenkins of Neath
1768	Iltid Thomas of Swansea
1769	Thomas Williams of Cowbridge
1770	Elias Jenkins of Swansea
1771	Thomas Williams of Cowbridge
1772	William Rees of St Mary Hill
1773	Iltid Thomas of Swansea
1774	Thomas Thomas of Cardiff
1775	Iltid Thomas of Swansea
1776	Thomas Thomas of Cardiff
1777	William Rees of St Mary Hill
1778	Iltid Thomas of Swansea
1779	William Rees of St Mary Hill

1780, 1781	Thomas Thomas of Cardiff
1782	Hopkin Llewellyn of Margam
1783	William Rees of St Mary Hill
1784	Thomas Thomas of Cardiff
1785	William Rees of St Mary Hill and of Court Colman
1786	Watkin Morgan of Llandough [-juxta-Cowbridge]
1787	John Wood of Cardiff
1788	Thomas Williams the elder of Cowbridge
1789	John Wood of Cardiff
1790	Hopkin Llewellyn, Gentleman, of Margam
1791	John Wood of Cardiff
1792	Hopkin Llewellyn, Gentleman
1793	Rees Davies of Swansea
1794	John Thomas of Cowbridge
1795	John Wood the elder of Cardiff
1796	William Vaughan, Wood's partner
1797	John Wood of Cardiff
1798	William Vaughan, Wood's partner
1799	Rees R. Williams of Cardiff
1800	John Wood of Cardiff
1801	Edward Davids, clerk to John Wood
1802	John Jeffreys of Swansea
1803	William Vaughan of Swansea
1804	John Wood the younger of Cardiff
1805	Edward Powell of Llantwit Major
1806	John Wood of Cardiff
1807	John Wood the younger
1808	Griffith Llewellyn of Baglan
1809	Wyndham Lewis of Cardiff
1810	John Jeffreys of Swansea
1811	Thomas Bassett of Boulson [Bonvilston]
1812	William Vaughan of Swansea
1813	Thomas Bassett of Boulson [Bonvilston]
1814	John Wood the younger of Cardiff
1815	Edward Priest Richards of Cardiff
1816	John Powell of Brecon
1817	Edward Priest Richards of Cardiff
1818	Lewis Thomas of Swansea
1819	John Jones of Brecon
1820	Edward Priest Richards
1821	William Meyrick of Merthyr Tydfil
1822	John James of Swansea
1823	William Meyrick of Merthyr Tydfil
1824	Thomas Bassett of Tresicking [Sigginston]
1825	Mr Thomas of Swansea
1826	Mr Thomas of Swansea

1827	John Jackson Price of Swansea
1828	Edward Priest Richards of Cardiff
1829	William Meyrick of Merthyr Tydfil
1830	David Powell of Neath
1831	Alexander Cuthbertson, Esquire, of Swansea
1832	William Lewis, Esquire, of Bridgend
1833	Alexander Cuthbertson of Neath
1834	David Powell, Esquire, of Neath
1835	Thomas Thomas, Esquire, of Swansea
1836	John Jenkins of Swansea
1837, 1838	John Gwyn Jeffreys, Esquire, of Swansea
1839–1841	Charles Basil Mansfield, Esquire, of Swansea
1842, 1843	John Gwyn Jeffreys, Esquire, of Swansea
1844	William Davies
1845, 1846	William Lewis
1847	Alexander Cuthbertson
1848, 1849	Thomas Evans
1850	Edward George Smith of Merthyr Tydfil
1851	William Lewis of Bridgend
1852	David Randall of Neath
1853	Alexander Cuthbertson
1854	David Randall of Neath
1855–1858	Richard Wyndham Williams
1859–1861	Thomas Masters Dalton [of Cardiff]
1862	Richard Wyndham Williams
1863	Alexander Cuthbertson
1864, 1865	John Morris
1866	Edward Strick of Swansea
1867	John Gaskoin of Swansea
1868, 1869	Richard Wyndham Williams of Cardiff
1870	Montague Grover of Cardiff
1871	James Kempthorne of Neath
1872	Richard Evans Spencer of Cardiff
1873	Lewis Vincent Shirley of Cardiff
1874–1876	Benjamin Matthews of Cardiff
1877–1884	Martin Scale of Neath
1885	Clement Waldron of Cardiff
1886	Martin Scale of Neath
1887	Walter Herbert Morgan of Pontypridd
1888, 1889	Rees Powell Morgan of Neath
1890	Walter Herbert Morgan of Pontypridd
1891, 1892	Rees Powell Morgan of Neath
1893	Edmund Bernard Reece of Cardiff
1894	Rees Powell Morgan of Neath
1895–1899	Lawrence Gardner Williams of Cardiff
1900–1904	David Isaac of Swansea

1904	George Gower Isaac of Swansea
1905	Henry Horatio Watkins of Swansea
1906	George Gower Isaac of Swansea
1907	Arthur Thomas Williams of Neath
1908	Henry Horatio Watkins of Swansea
1909	George Gower Isaac of Swansea
1910	Charles Joseph Clayton Wilson of Neath
1911	George Gower Isaac of Swansea
1912	Henry Horatio Watkins of Swansea
1913–1916	George Gower Isaac of Swansea
1916, 1917	Henry Horatio Watkins of Swansea
1918	Henry Thomas Box of Cardiff
1919, 1920	Henry Horatio Watkins of Swansea
1921–1923	Lawrence Gardner Williams of Cardiff
1924	Arthur Waldron of Cardiff
1925, 1926	Charles Joseph Clayton Wilson of Swansea
1927	Ernest Edward Green of Cardiff
1928	Charles Joseph Clayton Wilson of Swansea
1929	Ernest Edward Green of Cardiff
1930	Gerald Trevor Bruce of Pontypridd
1931	Ernest Edward Green of Cardiff
1932, 1933	Gerald Trevor Bruce of Cardiff
1934	Ernest Edward Green of Cardiff
1935, 1936	Gerald Trevor Bruce of Cardiff
1937	Ernest Edward Green of Cardiff
1938	Gerald Trevor Bruce of Cardiff
1939	Ernest Edward Green of Cardiff
1940	Edward Walter Hammond of Cardiff
1941, 1942	Ernest Edward Green of Cardiff
1943	Edward Walter Hammond of Cardiff
1944–1951	Ernest Edward Green of Cardiff
1952–1974	Francis Henry Gaskell of Cardiff

Under Sheriffs of the Bailiwick of Glamorgan

1974–1985	Francis Henry Gaskell of Cardiff
1985–1994	John Alcwyn Otto-Jones of Cardiff

Under Sheriffs of the Bailiwick of Swansea

1974–1983	Francis d'Aubeville Wilson of Swansea
1983–1994	John Humphrey Edmund of Swansea